Bertrand Russell
An Introduction

Bertrand Russell
An Introduction

Edited Selections from his Writings

BRIAN CARR
BA, M Phil,
Lecturer in Philosophy, University of Exeter

London   George Allen & Unwin Ltd
Ruskin House   Museum Street

ISBN 0 04 192032 5 hardback
0 04 192033 3 paperback

Printed in Great Britain
in 11 *point Times Roman type*
by Clarke, Doble & Brendon Ltd
Plymouth

To my parents
Wilfred and Gertrude Carr

Great spirits have always found violent opposition from mediocrities. The latter cannot understand when a man does not thoughtlessly submit to hereditary prejudices but honestly and courageously uses his intelligence.

ALBERT EINSTEIN

Preface

The primary aim in collecting together these selections from Bertrand Russell's books and papers, and presenting them in this particular manner, has been to provide a basis for group discussion classes in secondary schools and comparable institutions. (The general reader, nevertheless, who wishes to learn from Russell's own words the ideas of Britain's most eminent philosopher and social commentator should also find this form of presentation valuable.) The choice of Bertrand Russell's works for consideration hardly needs a justification here: his topics have an undeniable perennial interest, and his clarity of expression and honest arguments should be an excellent example of the way such subjects can be treated. It is no disadvantage in a book of this kind that his views are often provocative and controversial, for it aims precisely at provoking thought and discussion.

As for the plan of the book, the General Introduction presents a synopsis of Russell's life and of his writings and activities as a social commentator. The selections are then divided into four main parts. Each of these begins with a short introduction in which I have tried to unify the selections by indicating connecting links between Russell's arguments and relating the chosen passages to other papers where he treats the same or associated themes. As a general policy I have made no attempt at detailed criticism: instead the introductory sections include a set of questions which are intended to indicate salient points at which a critical consideration may begin. At the end of each part I have included also some suggestions on further readings from both Russell and other writers, and here I have tried to be helpful rather than exhaustive.

The final part of the collection, formed by extracts from papers in which Russell discusses some traditional philosophical problems, requires a separate comment. Philosophy is very rarely treated at the secondary educational stage, and I hope that this section may thus serve as something of an introduction to that unique discipline. The character of these extracts demands a departure from the general policy followed in the introductory passages, and the introduction to this section includes a closer examination of Russell's words. It also contains a general synopsis of Russell's writings on philosophical topics.

In the very limited space available it has obviously been impossible to do anything like justice to more than a few of Russell's many themes. In particular, if this book could have been longer, it would have included a section devoted to Russell's writings on sex, marriage, and morals. As it is, I can only recommend Russell's own *Marriage and Morals* as worthy of the most careful consideration. Limited space is responsible again for a further regrettable omission, this time from an area actually covered in the book: if space had allowed, something would have been included from Russell's philosophical autobiography, *My Philosophical Development*.

For permission to reprint these selections acknowledgements are due to the Russell Estate and to George Allen & Unwin Ltd. Acknowledgements are also due to the Clarendon Press, Oxford, for permission to include parts of *The Problems of Philosophy*.

I would like to record my gratitude to Lady Russell who did me the honour of reading the manuscript and making a number of useful suggestions and comments. I would like also to thank Professor Dan O'Connor for his encouragement of this project and for reading and commenting on a large part of the book; these are just a few of the many kindnesses he has shown me while I have been in Exeter. Throughout the preparation of the book invaluable help has been provided by Patrick Gallagher of Allen & Unwin, and my wife has done all in her power to make my task a lighter one.

Contents

General Introduction

Bertrand Russell, who became the third Earl Russell on his brother's death in 1931, was perhaps the most famous philosopher of this century. It is not often fully appreciated that the common man's notion of a philosopher is somewhat different from the one that pertains to the philosopher found in academic life in the universities. A philosopher, to the common man, is one who devotes his life to the important and deep problems that trouble mankind, problems such as the conflict between men's personal liberty and the constraints of authority, the adequacy and justification of our accepted modes of moral behaviour, and the difficult questions concerning the truth and social effects of religion. Bertrand Russell was certainly a philosopher in that sense, and as the common man's philosopher received the lasting admiration of his audience throughout the world. But Russell was also a philosopher in the stricter, academic sense, who achieved eminence early in this century through his original and brilliant work on matters that concern the common man but little; he has had a very great influence on the way the discipline of philosophy is practised in the universities of the Western world. I shall try to give some account of the nature of Russell's contributions to academic philosophy later,[1] but in this General Introduction I shall give an account of his life and work as a commentator on political and social problems.

FAMILY AND EDUCATION

Russell was born in 1872, on 18 May; he died at the age of ninety-seven on 2 February 1970. During his very distinguished life he produced more than fifty books, innumerable articles, broadcasts and lectures, and travelled and taught in a number of foreign countries; among his public honours were the Order of Merit in 1949, the Nobel Prize for Literature in 1950, in 1957 the UNESCO Kalinga Prize, and in 1960 the Danish Sonning Prize for contributions to European Culture. His ancestors were not themselves

---

[1] See the Introduction to Part Four.

undistinguished: his grandfather, Lord John Russell (the first Earl Russell), had twice been Prime Minister in the mid-nineteenth century; his father, Viscount Amberley, and his mother, the daughter of the second Lord Stanley of Alderley, were prominent through their support of such progressive movements as female suffrage. Both Russell's parents died before he was three, and he went with his brother Frank to live with their grandparents at Pembroke Lodge in Richmond Park, in spite of the fact that their father had appointed two free-thinkers as their guardians. Russell's grandmother, a daughter of the second Earl of Minto, was a person of strong moral and religious convictions, and had an important formative influence on his character; Frank was sent away to school, but Bertrand remained to be taught by private tutors at Pembroke Lodge.

At sixteen he was sent to an army crammer to prepare for a scholarship examination at Trinity College, Cambridge. He obtained the scholarship and went up to Trinity in 1890 to read mathematics. Thus began his lifelong association with that College. After three years he was placed Seventh Wrangler in the Mathematical Tripos, and remained for a further year to study philosophy, being awarded a First with Distinction in the Moral Science Tripos. He became a Fellow at Trinity the following year, a position he held until 1901, in 1899 giving a course of lectures on Leibniz which formed the substance of one of his first philosophical books. In 1910 Russell was to return again to take up a post as Lecturer in Philosophy on a five-year contract, which unhappily was not renewed: because of his pacifist activities during the First World War, and his appearance in court as a result of them, the College Council decided not to reappoint him, though most of the younger Fellows spoke up on his behalf. However, with the end of the war came a change of heart, and he was reinstated as a Fellow in 1919, though for various reasons he did not take up his duties again at Trinity until 1944. Four years later, in 1948, his Fellowship was converted to one that carried no teaching commitments and that he held for life.

EARLY TRAVELS AND WRITINGS

For some months in 1894 Russell worked in Paris as an attaché at the British Embassy. On returning to England he married Alys Pearsall Smith, and since he did not need to be in residence at

Cambridge they decided to visit Germany, where Russell attended Berlin University. He used this opportunity to acquaint himself with the ideas of the Social Democrats, 'who were at that time considered very wicked', and the outcome of his visit was *German Social Democracy* (1896). In later years Russell spent time in Russia and China, and similarly published accounts of the social and political problems those countries faced: *The Practice and Theory of Bolshevism* (1920), and *The Problem of China* (1922). Russell made the trip to Russia in order to see at first hand the changes instigated by the Communists, and was able to meet Lenin, Trotsky and Gorky. Though the British Socialists thought it wrong at the time to criticise the Bolsheviks openly, Russell saw fit to publish his verdict; admitting to a sympathy with the aims of Bolshevism, he could not accept their methods, or the final submission of the individual to the State. He was indeed more impressed by pre-revolutionary China, where he spent a year at the invitation of the Chinese Lecture Association teaching at the National University of Peking. He was accompanied to China by Dora Black, who became his second wife in 1921.

By that time Russell had already begun his many visits to the United States. In 1896 he went with Alys to meet her American relatives, and spent some months giving lectures at Bryn Mawr College and Johns Hopkins University. In 1914 he gave the Lowell Lectures at Boston, and was a temporary lecturer at Harvard University: among the many acquaintances he made there was the young T. S. Eliot, then a postgraduate student of his. In the 1920s he undertook a number of lecture tours in America. In the 1920s also Russell devoted himself in earnest to literary works, publishing some of his most popular and most controversial books. Among these were his trenchant criticism of religious belief, *Why I am Not a Christian* (1927), which later was included in a collection under that general title edited by Paul Edwards (1957); *Sceptical Essays* (1928), composed of papers on a variety of subjects including the problem of freedom and authority, with the general theme of the need for tolerance and rationality in human affairs; *Marriage and Morals* (1929), in which he treats of the origins and failings of the current sexual code, and discusses possible improvements for the sake of human happiness and well-being; and *The Conquest of Happiness* (1930), where he attempts a diagnosis of modern man's loss of 'the zest for life'. In this decade

Russell also produced *The Prospects of Industrial Civilisation* (1923) (with Dora Black as co-author), and two popular works on science, *ABC of Atoms* (1923) and *ABC of Relativity* (1925).

THE NEW YORK INCIDENT

Russell went again to America in 1938 to lecture at the University of Chicago, and then in the following year at the University of California. In 1940 he accepted an invitation to teach philosophy at the City College of New York, resigning his appointment at California to take up this post, but then occurred the extraordinary lawsuit of a certain Mrs Kay who succeeded in getting the appointment revoked. (The details of this episode are revealed in Paul Edwards's appendix to his 1957 edition of *Why I am Not a Christian*.[2]) When the appointment was made public, a Bishop Manning of the Protestant Episcopal Church led the attack by denouncing Russell in all the New York newspapers; Mrs Kay then brought her case against the City College ostensibly to protect her daughter from Russell's immoral influence (notwithstanding the fact that he was to teach academic subjects, and the college accepted only male students). Her action was vociferously supported by the Catholic newspapers and dignitaries of New York, and though many prominent academics and spokesmen of more liberal religious groups took up Russell's public defence, the case was heard by Judge McGeehan, a Catholic (who, writes Edwards, already 'had distinguished himself by trying to have a portrait of Martin Luther removed from a courthouse mural illustrating legal history'). McGeehan revoked the appointment on three grounds: firstly, that Russell was an alien; secondly, that he had not been given a competitive examination; and thirdly, because of the 'immoral and salacious doctrines' that he preached. Russell himself was not allowed to take part in the proceedings, nor was he given the chance to reply publicly in the newspapers to such ridiculous charges as that he and his wife paraded naked in public and that he went in for salacious poetry. Harvard University had invited him to give a series of lectures, and bravely stood by this commitment; but as a result of the case Russell found it difficult to earn enough

[2] See also B. Feinberg and R. Kasrils, *Bertrand Russell's America*, vol. I (Allen & Unwin 1973).

to support his family in America. He was finally saved by an invitation to teach at the Barnes Foundation, and an advance of some value for his forthcoming *History of Western Philosophy*. He did return to America again in 1950 to Columbia University, where, as Edwards relates, in contrast to this unsavoury affair 'he was given a rousing reception which those who were present are not likely to forget'.

THE BEACON HILL EXPERIMENT

Some of the ideas that resulted in the New York incident had been set forth in Russell's book *On Education* (1926), which seems in retrospect a wholly admirable and level-headed work. These ideas, however, were so revolutionary in the twenties that Russell and Dora Black decided in 1927 to open their own private school as the only hope of giving their own two children, John and Kate, an adequate educational environment. Beacon Hill School was set up in Frank Russell's house on the South Downs. 'We wanted,' Russell wrote, 'an unusual combination: on the one hand, we disliked prudery and religious instruction and a great many restraints on freedom which are taken for granted in conventional schools; on the other hand, we could not agree with "modern" educationists in thinking scholastic instruction unimportant, or in advocating a *complete* absence of discipline.'[3] The school was unfortunately not a real success, making large claims on their time and financial resources; indeed many of Russell's writings at that time, and the American lecture tours, were undertaken to provide the necessary money. Further, the school attracted a fair number of problem children, and Russell had great trouble in effecting his idea of the right balance between freedom and discipline. The school continued in Dora's hands into the 1940s, though Russell left it in 1932 when his marriage with Dora broke up. In that year he also published his excellent *Education and the Social Order,* where he treats of the social pressures preventing the recognition of the individual's rights in present educational practice. In 1938 he married his third wife, Patricia Helen Spence, who had been a teacher at Beacon Hill, and his second son, Conrad, was born the following year.

[3] *Autobiography of Bertrand Russell*, vol. III, p. 152.

B

FIRST WORLD WAR, POLITICS, AND PACIFISM

For two periods in his life, Russell was prominent through his activities in public affairs. The second of these ran from the end of the Second World War to his death in 1970; the first was concentrated around his pacifist activities during the First World War. Before 1914 he had twice attempted, unsuccessfully, to become elected to Parliament, in 1907 at a by-election in Wimbledon as a candidate for the 'National Union of Women's Suffrage Societies', and in 1910 when he missed the chance of being Liberal candidate for Bedford through his open disavowal of religious belief. After the First World War, in 1923 and in the following year, he stood unsuccessfully as Labour candidate for Chelsea. His political associates before the war included the Fabians, of whom H. G. Wells, George Bernard Shaw, and Sidney and Beatrice Webb were the leading figures. But Russell first became a prominent public figure through his work with the No Conscription Fellowship (or NCF), the main organisation for pacifist propaganda. (He also at that time formed a short-lived friendship with D. H. Lawrence, who for his own peculiar reasons was an opponent of the war.)

With England in the grip of war fever, Russell's speeches and writings in favour of capitulation to the Germans[4] raised considerable public hostility, and in common with a number of dissenting intellectuals he incurred the disfavour of the authorities. He was responsible for a pamphlet, issued by the NCF, denouncing the harsh punishment of a conscientious objector; the result was a trial in June 1916 at which he was found guilty of 'statements likely to prejudice the recruiting of His Majesty's Forces'. He was fined £100, and the report of his speech at the trial and the court proceedings, issued by the NCF, was suppressed; further, he was refused a passport to take up an invitation to lecture at Harvard and was banned from giving lectures in the 'prohibited areas' (the coastal towns) of Britain for security reasons. The worst consequence of this episode, as far as Russell was concerned, was the loss of his position at Trinity. A second and equally unfortunate clash with the authorities resulted from an article he wrote for the NCF weekly, *Tribunal*, a short time later: in the course of explaining the probable outcome of a continuation of the war, he made

[4] See e.g. Chap. 7.

reference to the behaviour of the American army in breaking strikes, and this sufficiently displeased the authorities for them to confine him in Brixton prison for a term of six months from May 1918. His confinement was not totally unpleasant, however, for his friends and relatives managed to get him into the First Division, where he was allowed enough comforts to continue his academic writings.

It was during the First World War that Russell also published the first of a number of books in which he attempted to arrive at some solution to the complex problem of freedom and the constraints of authority. This was *Principles of Social Reconstruction* (1916), a work that still has great value today. Here Russell divides human impulses into the possessive and the creative; the State, war, and property are the chief political embodiments of the possessive impulses and marriage, education, and religion ought to embody the creative ones. 'I consider the best life that which is most built on creative impulses,' he wrote. 'Liberation of creativeness ought to be the principle of reform both in politics and economics.' Many of his suggestions occurred again in *Roads to Freedom: Socialism, Anarchism and Syndicalism* (1918), where he accepts a form of Socialism, Guild Socialism, as representing the best embodiment of a solution. Among his later treatments of this problem were: *Freedom and Organisation 1814–1914* (1934); *Power: A New Social Analysis* (1938); the BBC Reith Lectures, *Authority and the Individual* (1949), where he stresses the complications of the problem in a society in which planning and control have become of great importance; and *Human Society in Ethics and Politics* (1954).

NUCLEAR DISARMAMENT AND THE PEACE FOUNDATION

The second period in his life when Russell was most active in public affairs began shortly after the end of the Second World War (also a time of deep personal happiness for him with his fourth wife, Edith Finch, whom he married in 1952). It was also during the early fifties that the importance of his works was recognised publicly in such awards as the Order of Merit and the Nobel Prize. '1950,' he later wrote, 'marked the apogee of my respectability.' Yet the respectability was not long-lived, for it was in the fifties that he began his attempts to stir up public awareness of the danger of a nuclear war and provoke governments into a saner course of action.[5]

Russell felt that the one hope left of escaping a world holocaust was the emergence of a single World Government, more urgent than ever since the bombing of Hiroshima and Nagasaki in 1945. He made a number of broadcasts during 1953,[6] emphasising the dangers inherent in the possession of nuclear devices, and followed them two years later with an appeal, signed jointly with Albert Einstein and a number of other leading world scientists, for government action to avert the dangers. In 1957 he instigated, and became the first president of, the Pugwash Conferences, which were attended by scientists of many countries (an immensely important achievement in itself) and were aimed at seeking ways in which those responsible for the atom and hydrogen bombs could exert some influence on those with the power to use them; these meetings had some success in bringing about a partial Test Ban Treaty. He became the president of the Campaign for Nuclear Disarmament movement, of which Canon Collins was chairman, and supported the famous Aldermaston marches of the late fifties. *Common Sense and Nuclear Warfare* (1959), and *Has Man a Future?* (1961) were written as part of this campaign. By 1960 Russell felt the need had come for more effective methods of stirring public demand for change in government policies, and he resigned from the CND to form the more militant Committee of 100, a movement for mass civil disobedience which held the Trafalgar Square Rally and sit-down at the Ministry of Defence in February 1961; the rally was attended by an estimated 20,000 people. On 'Hiroshima Day', 6 August of that year, they held a second rally at Hyde Park; on this occasion Russell and his wife, with other members of the Committee of 100, were held responsible for inciting civil disobedience. He and his wife were sentenced to two months in prison, commuted to seven days on medical grounds.

At the time of the Cuban missile crisis of October 1962, and the Sino-Indian border dispute a few months later, Russell exerted whatever influence he could to bring about peaceful settlements.

---

[5] The details of Russell's activities at this time are fully documented in *Autobiography of Bertrand Russell*, vol. III.

[6] Including the famous 'Man's Peril' broadcast – see Egner and Denonn (eds), *The Basic Writings of Bertrand Russell*.

He refrained from taking sides in either dispute, and on the whole his communications with U Thant and the heads of states involved were well received; the Western press was hardly as sympathetic, apparently regarding with suspicion someone who could see any force in the claims of Communist regimes. (Russell's letters, and the replies he received, are included in *Unarmed Victory* (1963) which documents his part in these two incidents.) However, the Cuban crisis did as much as the CND and the Committee of 100 to stimulate dissatisfaction with current international politics, and Russell's idea of an international body for seeking peaceful solutions to such disputes had an encouraging response; the Bertrand Russell Peace Foundation, which included in its list of sponsors such eminent men as Albert Schweitzer and Linus Pauling, was inaugurated in 1963.[7] Russell was of course aware that the task undertaken by the Foundation ought to have been the responsibility of the United Nations Organisation, but he saw the exclusion of China from the United Nations and the existence of undemocratic veto powers as barriers to any successful functioning of that organisation, and a hindrance, along with its lack of military power to enforce its decisions, to its ideal function as a World Government.

While continuing his work with the Peace Foundation, and taking up the cause of political prisoners and persecuted minorities throughout the world, Russell further risked the charge of being a Communist sympathiser by becoming a prominent opponent of American involvement in Vietnam. In the mid-sixties he came to view the continuation of the Vietnam war as the chief threat to world security, and the methods employed by the Americans in their prosecution of the war little improvement on those that had resulted in the Nuremberg trials. The Foundation had sent observers to Vietnam and Russell believed that their reports justified the strongest possible action: he appealed to American soldiers in May 1966 over the National Liberation Front radio for an end to 'this barbarous and criminal war of conquest'; he published his indictment of American policy in *War Crimes in Vietnam* (1967); and finally, supported by a number of other internationally famous figures, he organised a War Crimes Tribunal for the purpose of

[7] See Russell's paper 'A New Approach to Peace', reprinted in *Autobiography of Bertrand Russell*, vol. III, pp. 179–87.

publicising and passing judgement on American methods and policy. As a result, the Peace Foundation lost some of the valuable support given a few years before, and in the eyes of at least some authorities Russell's respectability was once again at a somewhat low ebb.

Chronological Chart of Russell's Life

1872 Born 18 May at Ravenscroft in Monmouthshire
1876 Moves with his brother Frank to Pembroke Lodge, home of his grandfather Lord John Russell
1890 Enters Trinity College, Cambridge
1894 Fellow at Trinity. Spends some months as attaché at British Embassy in Paris. First marriage, to Alys Pearsall Smith
1895 Visits Germany. Writes *German Social Democracy*
1896 Visits United States with Alys. Lectures at Johns Hopkins University and Bryn Mawr College
1903 Publishes *The Principles of Mathematics*
1910 Publishes (with A. N. Whitehead) *Principia Mathematica*. Lecturer in Philosophy at Trinity
1914 Delivers Lowell Lectures, *Our Knowledge of the External World*, in Boston. Lectures at Harvard University
1916 NCF pamphlet on Everett case results in £100 fine. Refused passport and loses Trinity post. Publishes *Principles of Social Reconstruction*
1918 Six months' imprisonment for *Tribunal* article. Publishes *Roads to Freedom*
1919 Reinstated at Trinity
1920 Visits Russia, meeting Lenin, Trotsky and Gorky. Publishes *The Practice and Theory of Bolshevism*
1921 Lectures at National University of Peking. Second marriage, to Dora Black. Publishes *The Analysis of Mind*
1924 Lecture tour in United States
1925 Delivers Tarner Lectures at Trinity, *The Analysis of Matter*
1926 Publishes *On Education*
1927 Opens Beacon Hill School. Publishes *Why I am Not a Christian*
1929 Publishes *Marriage and Morals*
1931 Becomes the third Earl Russell
1932 Leaves Beacon Hill. Publishes *Education and the Social Order*
1936 Third marriage, to Patricia Helen Spence

1938   Lectures at University of Chicago. Publishes *Power: A New Social Analysis*

1939   Lectures at University of California

1940   Appointment at the City College of New York revoked. Lectures at Harvard University

1941   Lectures at the Barnes Foundation, Pennsylvania

1944   Returns to Trinity

1946   Publishes *History of Western Philosophy*

1949   Awarded the Order of Merit. Delivers BBC Reith Lectures, *Authority and the Individual*

1950   Receives Nobel Prize for Literature. Visits Australia. Lectures at Columbia University

1952   Fourth marriage, to Edith Finch

1953   BBC broadcasts appealing for nuclear disarmament

1955   Appeals with Einstein and others for nuclear disarmament

1957   Awarded the Kalinga Prize by UNESCO. Instigates the Pugwash Conferences

1958   President of the Campaign for Nuclear Disarmament movement

1959   Publishes *Common Sense and Nuclear Warfare*, and *My Philosophical Development*

1960   Awarded the Danish Sonning Prize. Founder member of Committee of 100

1961   Seven days' imprisonment in Brixton for Hyde Park Rally

1963   Bertrand Russell Peace Foundation inaugurated

1966   Appeals to American soldiers for end of Vietnam war. Opens the War Crimes Tribunal

1967   Publishes *War Crimes in Vietnam*

1970   Dies 2 February, aged 97

Part One

Authority and Liberty

Introduction

THE CONFLICT OF EFFICIENCY AND INITIATIVE

As we have seen, Russell was throughout his life a champion of liberty against authoritarian government – in his defence of conscientious objectors, of religious tolerance and of freedom from political persecution. Though he wrote much on these themes, there is one *general* problem (of which these are but aspects) which he again and again addressed in his socio-political writings: the complex and difficult conflict between the demands on the one hand, for an efficient form of government, and on the other hand, for the greatest degree of personal liberty and opportunity for initiative. Now Russell took it as axiomatic that any solution to the problem must give the greatest possible weight to the demand for liberty, for without freedom and initiative (some voice in the political and industrial circumstances of life) not only is personal happiness forfeit but also the vitality and growth of society itself. (See 'The State',[1] 'Control and Initiative' and Chapter 3.) Nevertheless, and it is this that creates the general problem in its most acute form, he recognised the necessity of government control over our lives and even argued for an increase of such control in industrial and financial affairs far beyond the level we are familiar with in the West. *Socialism*, that is state ownership and control of industry and finance, he thought was necessary for the efficient use of resources and manpower in a scientific age, but the immediate effect of central organisation is to make man 'a cog in the machine': 'Scientific technique, by making society more organic, increases the extent to which an individual is a cog; if it is not to be an evil, ways must be found of preventing him from being a *mere* cog. This means that initiative must be preserved in spite of organisation.'[2]

GUILD SOCIALISM

It is obvious that this problem does not admit of an easy solution;

[1] For full references to this and other papers mentioned see the list of Further Readings on p. 56.
[2] See Chap. 3.

there must be central control for efficiency, and yet there must be freedom and opportunity for initiative to ensure vitality and growth. Russell offered as the best solution a form of Socialism, Guild Socialism, which is calculated to give effective voice in industry to the individual worker. Whether this does in fact solve the problem will be taken up later, but for the moment we must see the nature of Guild Socialism, and try to understand the complete argument in its favour. The guiding idea of Guild Socialism is that, once the primary functions of the State have been met, responsibility for organising ways and means of production is allowed to devolve onto the workers themselves. Each factory controls its methods of production by means of elected managers, and all factories in a given industry are federated into a National Guild to deal with marketing and the general interests of that industry. In return for its raw materials and machinery the Guild pays a tax to the State, and the profits of production are apportioned among its members. The ultimate governing body of the society is a joint Committee of Parliament comprising the Parliament of geographically elected representatives and the Guild Congress. (See *Roads to Freedom*, pages 64 ff., as well as Chapter 1 of this book.)

THE ARGUMENT FOR GUILD SOCIALISM

To see clearly the complete argument establishing Guild Socialism as the ideal form of society we must work upwards from very basic questions. The argument includes a consideration of such questions as: Why have *any* form of government at all? What *functions* should government have? What economic arguments exist for a *Socialist* form of government? Why should a society be *democratic*?

1. *Anarchism or government?* 'Government and law', writes Russell, 'in their very essence, consist of restrictions on freedom, and freedom is the greatest of political goods' (see Chapter 1). It might be thought, therefore, that our conflict between authority and liberty should be settled solely in favour of the latter in some system like that suggested by such Anarchists as Bakunin and Kropotkin, where coercion by the community is unnecessary and social life is based upon free agreement. In his elegant criticism of this idea, Russell shows that certain limitations on freedom are

in any event unavoidable. Even in an Anarchist society, *some* acts must be forbidden by law: theft, crimes of violence, and the creation of organisations intended to subvert the Anarchist regime are the most obvious.

2. *The functions of government.* Is it possible to state a *general* principle dividing those spheres of life where government should exert authority from those where individual initiative may be allowed to operate? In 'Control and Initiative: Their Respective Spheres' Russell suggests that such a principle may be stated in terms of the different kinds of impulses that make up human nature.

> On the one hand, we have impulses to hold what we possess, and (too often) to acquire what others possess. On the other hand, we have creative impulses, impulses to put something into the world which is not taken away from anybody else. . . . Broadly speaking, the regularisation of possessive impulses and their control by the law belong to the *essential* functions of government, while the creative impulses, though governments may encourage them, should derive their main influence from individual or group autonomy.[3]

3. *The economic necessity of Socialism.* The consideration often advanced for Socialism is that justice requires a more equitable distribution of wealth and economic power than is found in Capitalist societies; Russell's argument for Socialism is rather different from this: 'For my part, while I am as convinced a Socialist as the most ardent Marxian, I do not regard Socialism as a gospel of proletarian revenge, nor even, *primarily*, as a means of securing economic justice. I regard it primarily as an adjustment to machine production demanded by considerations of common sense.'[4] Socialism consists in state ownership of ultimate economic power, involving at least the control of land and minerals, capital, banking, and foreign trade. Only by such control can the planning necessary for economic use of resources and manpower be undertaken: in a Socialist society industries do not compete for greater profits, but

[3] 'Control and Initiative', p. 79.
[4] 'The Case for Socialism', p. 76.

instead each industry is conducted for the benefit of the nation as a whole.

4. *Democracy as a safeguard*. Socialism, however, may easily be accompanied by many unwanted evils. The shortcomings of State Socialism are enumerated in 'Control and Initiative': if the State is to have control over the publishing industry this may mean a strict enforcement of censorship on every type of anti-government opinion; if the State controls education this probably implies another most effective means of propaganda; the State can, if it controls all important institutions, demand political orthodoxy of all who seek positions of responsibility – the evils, indeed, that are often charged against the present State Socialism of Russia and other Communist states. Russell was most concerned to stress these evils, and they form a great part in his rejection of State Socialism as an ideal of government. (See, for example, *The Practice and Theory of Bolshevism*.) In 'The Taming of Power' (Chapter 2 below) Russell identifies the mistake that State Socialists make in putting their hopes for man's liberation in their particular doctrine, as the failure to recognise the difference between ownership and control of economic power: the dispossession of the Capitalist is not sufficient for the liberation of man, for in itself it may easily lead to a tyranny of the State over its citizens. 'If concentration of power in a single organisation – the State – is not to produce the evils of despotism in an extreme form, it is essential that power within the organisation should be widely distributed, and that subordinate groups should have a large measure of autonomy.'[5] In sum, the argument for democracy given here is for democracy as a safeguard against evils likely to attend a State Socialism.

5. *Democracy as opportunity for initiative*. It would be mistaken, nevertheless, to regard this as the conclusion of the argument for Guild Socialism. Certainly the argument as stated indicates the necessity (on economic ground) of *Socialism*, and the need for *democratic* control of the State's economic power. However, Guild Socialism is concerned to *defend democracy itself* against the autocratic power of the State, and the argument as stated so far represents democracy as itself a safeguard against such power – indeed in the conception of Guild Socialism the idea of democracy,

[5] 'The Taming of Power', p. 197.

in the sense of opportunity for personal initiative (in many aspects of life, but most importantly in the citizen having a voice in decisions concerning affairs of the State and of industry) is an idea of something far more important than simply a safeguard against the evils of autocratic power. The all-important point is that Guild Socialism provides for each and every citizen an opportunity to contribute to society and hence to exercise a degree of creativeness. 'The most important purpose that political institutions can achieve is to keep alive in individuals creativeness, vigour, vitality, and the joy of life.'[6] Guild Socialism is meant to return to the individual some measure of initiative, to relieve him of the burden of being *merely* a cog in a machine. (This final part of the argument is clearest in Chapter 3 below.)

COMMENTS

Russell's writings on Guild Socialism raise a large number of interesting and important questions, and it can hardly be denied that he presents the leading ideas in an attractive light. However, there do seem to be a number of points in the argument which deserve close scrutiny, and I mention here just a few.

Russell's argument for Socialism. If, as Russell says, society has become such that central planning and control are important for efficiency, does it follow that *State* control is the only possibility? An alternative would appear to be control by a confederation of private industries – if economic considerations are *all* that matter (one is not taking account, for example, of considerations of economic justice), there would seem little to choose between these alternatives.

Guild Socialism. Though the idea of Guild Socialism is admirable as an embodiment of economic and political justice, in relation to the conflicting demands of control and initiative it hardly seems to be a solution. Indeed devolution of power in this fashion, though meeting one demand, would seem simply to ignore the need for *central* planning and control, and to produce little in the way of a compromise solution.

Secondly, Guild Socialism would not obviously result in the

[6] 'Property', p. 93.

harmony of economic aspirations of all workers, for just as private industries have competed for profit, and just as trade unions are primarily interested in the well-being of their own members, different Guilds would retain the profit motive in relation to workers in that industry. As the Webbs wrote in criticism of the Guild Socialism idea:

> Each vocation, however large and important it may be, is but a fragment of the community. The commodities and services that it turns out are, almost entirely, not for consumption or use by its own members, but for consumption and use by the rest of the community. Hence the self-governing workshop, or the self-governing industry, necessarily producing for exchange, is perpetually tempted to make a profit on cost.[7]

QUESTIONS

1. In what ways can a man's freedom be justifiably restricted?
2. What is government for?
3. Is it possible for majority rule to conflict with democracy?
4. What relationship exists between democracy and Socialism? Is it possible to have one without the other?

[7] Quoted from Coates and Topham (eds), *Workers' Control*, p. 68.

Chapter 1

Government and Law[1]

Government and law, in their very essence, consist of restrictions on freedom, and freedom is the greatest of political goods. A hasty reasoner might conclude without further ado that law and government are evils which must be abolished if freedom is our goal. But this consequence, true or false, cannot be proved so simply. In this chapter we shall examine the arguments of Anarchists against law and the State. We shall proceed on the assumption that freedom is the supreme aim of a good social system; but on this very basis we shall find the Anarchist contentions very questionable.

Respect for the liberty of others is not a natural impulse with most men: envy and love of power lead ordinary human nature to find pleasure in interferences with the lives of others. If all men's actions were wholly unchecked by external authority, we should not obtain a world in which all men would be free. The strong would oppress the weak, or the majority would oppress the minority, or the lovers of violence would oppress the more peaceable people. I fear it cannot be said that these bad impulses are *wholly* due to a bad social system, though it must be conceded that the present competitive organisation of society does a great deal to foster the worst elements in human nature. The love of power is an impulse which, though innate in very ambitious men, is chiefly promoted as a rule by the actual experience of power. In a world where none could acquire much power, the desire to tyrannise would be much less strong than it is at present. Nevertheless, I cannot think that it would be wholly absent, and those in whom it would exist would often be men of unusual energy and executive capacity. Such men, if they are not restrained by the organised will of the community, may either succeed in establishing a despotism, or, at any rate, make such a vigorous attempt as can only be be defeated through a period of prolonged disturbance.

[1] From *Roads to Freedom* (1918), pp. 82–7.

C

And apart from the love of political power, there is the love of power over individuals. If threats and terrorism were not prevented by law, it can hardly be doubted that cruelty would be rife in the relations of men and women and of parents and children. It is true that the habits of a community can make such cruelty rare, but these habits, I fear, are only to be produced through the prolonged reign of law. Experience of backwood communities, mining camps, and other such places seems to show that under new conditions men easily revert to a more barbarous attitude and practice. It would seem, therefore, that, while human nature remains as it is, there will be more liberty for all in a community where some acts of tyranny by individuals are forbidden, than in a community where the law leaves each individual free to follow his every impulse. But, although the necessity of some form of government and law must for the present be conceded, it is important to remember that all law and government is in itself in some degree an evil, only justifiable when it prevents other and greater evils. Every use of the power of the State needs, therefore, to be very closely scrutinised, and every possibility of diminishing its power is to be welcomed provided it does not lead to a reign of private tyranny.

The power of the State is partly legal, partly economic: acts of a kind which the State dislikes can be punished by the criminal law, and individuals who incur the displeasure of the State may find it hard to earn a livelihood.

The views of Marx on the State are not very clear. On the one hand he seems willing, like the modern State Socialists, to allow great power to the State, but on the other hand he suggests that when the Socialist revolution has been consummated, the State, as we know it, will disappear. Among the measures which are advocated in the Communist Manifesto as immediately desirable, there are several which would very greatly increase the power of the existing State – for example, 'Centralisation of credit in the hands of the State, by means of a national bank with state capital and an exclusive monopoly'; and again, 'Centralisation of the means of communication and transport in the hands of the State'. But the Manifesto goes on to say:

When, in the course of development, class distinctions have disappeared, and all production has been concentrated in the hands of a vast association of the whole nation, the public power will lose its political character. Political power, properly so called, is merely the organised power of one class for oppressing another. If the proletariat during its contest with the bourgeoisie is compelled, by the force of circumstances, to organise itself as a class, if, by means of a revolution, it makes itself the ruling class, and, as such, sweeps away by force the old conditions of production, then it will, along with these conditions, have swept away the conditions for the existence of class antagonisms, and of classes generally, and will thereby have abolished its own supremacy as a class.

In place of the old bourgeois society, with its classes and class antagonisms, we shall have an association, in which the free development of each is the condition for the free development of all.[2]

This attitude Marx preserved in essentials throughout his life. Accordingly it is not to be wondered at that his followers, so far as regards their immediate aims, have in the main become out-and-out State Socialists. On the other hand, the Syndicalists who accept from Marx the doctrine of the class war, which they regard as what is really vital in his teaching, reject the State with abhorrence and wish to abolish it wholly, in which respect they are at one with the Anarchists. The Guild Socialists, though some persons in this country regard them as extremists, really represent the English love of compromise. The Syndicalist arguments as to the dangers inherent in the power of the State have made them dissatisfied with the old State Socialism, but they are unable to accept the Anarchist view that society can dispense altogether with a central authority. Accordingly they propose that there should be two co-equal instruments of government in a community, the one geographical, representing the consumers, and essentially the continuation of the democratic State, the other representing the producers, organised, not geographically, but in guilds, after the manner of industrial unionism. These two authorities will deal with different classes of questions. Guild Socialists do not regard the industrial authority as forming part of the State, for they contend that it is the essence of the State to be geographical; but the industrial authority will resemble the present State in the fact that it will

[2] *Communist Manifesto* (1848), p. 22.

have coercive powers, and that its decrees will be enforced, when necessary. It is to be suspected that Syndicalists also, much as they object to the existing State, would not object to coercion of individuals in an industry by the Trade Union in that industry. Government within the Trade Union would probably be quite as strict as state government is now. In saying this we are assuming that the theoretical anarchism of Syndicalist leaders would not survive accession to power, but I am afraid experience shows that this is not a very hazardous assumption.

Among all these different views, the one which raises the deepest issue is the Anarchist contention that all coercion by the community is unnecessary. Like most of the things that Anarchists say, there is much more to be urged in support of this view than most people would suppose at first sight. Kropotkin, who is its ablest exponent, points out how much has been achieved already by the method of free agreement. He does not wish to abolish government in the sense of collective decisions: what he does wish to abolish is the system by which a decision is enforced upon those who oppose it. The whole system of representative government and majority rule is to him a bad thing. He points to such instances as the agreements among the different railway systems of the Continent for the running of through expresses and for co-operation generally. He points out that in such cases the different companies or authorities concerned each appoint a delegate, and that the delegates suggest a basis of agreement, which has to be subsequently ratified by each of the bodies appointing them. The assembly of delegates has no coercive power whatever, and a majority can do nothing against a recalcitrant minority. Yet this has not prevented the conclusion of very elaborate systems of agreements. By such methods, so Anarchists contend, the *useful* functions of government can be carried out without any coercion. They maintain that the usefulness of agreement is so patent as to make co-operation certain if once the predatory motives associated with the present system of private property were removed.

Attractive as this view is, I cannot resist the conclusion that it results from impatience and represents the attempt to find a short cut towards the ideal which all human people desire.

Let us begin with the question of private crime. Anarchists maintain that the criminal is manufactured by bad social conditions and would disappear in such a world as they aim at creating. No doubt there is a great measure of truth in this view. There would be little motive to robbery, for example, in an Anarchist world unless it were organised on a large scale by a body of men bent on upsetting the Anarchists' regime. It may also be conceded that impulses towards criminal violence could be very largely eliminated by a better education. But all such contentions, it seems to me, have their limitations. To take an extreme case, we cannot suppose that there would be no lunatics in an Anarchist community, and some of these lunatics would, no doubt, be homicidal. Probably no one would argue that they ought to be left at liberty. But there are no sharp lines in nature: from the homicidal lunatic to the sane man of violent passions there is a continuous gradation. Even in the most perfect community there will be men and women, otherwise sane, who will feel an impulse to commit murder from jealousy. These are now usually restrained by the fear of punishment, but if this fear were removed, such murders would probably become much more common, as may be seen from the present behaviour of certain soldiers on leave. Moreover, certain kinds of conduct arouse public hostility, and would almost inevitably lead to lynching, if no other recognised method of punishment existed. There is in most men a certain natural vindictiveness, not always directed against the worst members of the community. For example, Spinoza was very nearly murdered by the mob because he was suspected of undue friendliness to France at a time when Holland was at war with that country. Apart from such cases, there would be the very real danger of an organised attempt to destroy Anarchism and revive ancient oppressions. Is it to be supposed, for example, that Napoleon, if he had been born into such a community as Kropotkin advocates, would have acquiesced tamely in a world where his genius could find no scope? I cannot see what should prevent a combination of ambitious men forming themselves into a private army, manufacturing their own munitions, and at last enslaving the defenceless citizens, who had relied upon the inherent attractiveness of liberty. It would not be consistent with the principles of Anarchism for the community to interfere with the drilling of a private army, no matter what its objects might be (though, of course, an opposing private army might be formed by men with different views). Indeed, Kropotkin instances the old Volunteers in Great Britain as an example of a movement on Anarchist lines. Even if a predatory army were not formed from within, it might easily come from a neighbouring nation, or from races on the borderland of civilisation. So long as the love of power exists, I do not see how it can be prevented from finding an outlet in oppression except by means of the organised force of the community.

Chapter 2

The Taming of Power[1]

'In passing by the side of Mount Thai, Confucius came on a woman who was weeping bitterly by a grave. The Master pressed forward and drove quickly to her; then he sent Tze-lu to question her. "Your wailing," said he, "is that of one who has suffered sorrow on sorrow." She replied, "That is so. Once my husband's father was killed here by a tiger. My husband was also killed, and now my son has died in the same way." The Master said, "Why do you not leave the place?" The answer was, "There is no oppressive government here." The Master then said, "Remember this, my children: oppressive government is more terrible than tigers." '

The subject of the present chapter is the problem of insuring that government shall be *less* terrible than tigers. . . .

I

The merits of democracy are negative: it does not insure good government, but it prevents certain evils. Until women began to take part in political affairs, married women had no control over their own property, or even over their own earnings; a char-woman with a drunken husband had no redress if he prevented her from using her wages for support of her children. The oligarchical Parliament of the eighteenth and early nineteenth centuries used its legislative power to increase the wealth of the rich by depressing the condition of both rural and urban labour. Only democracy has prevented the law from making trade unionism impossible. But for democracy, Western America, Australia, and New Zealand would be inhabited by a semi-servile yellow population governed by a small white aristocracy. The evils of slavery and serfdom are familiar, and wherever a minority has a secure monopoly of political power, the majority is likely to sink, sooner or later, into either

[1] From *Power: A New Social Analysis* (1938), pp. 185–96.

slavery or serfdom. All history shows that, as might be expected, minorities cannot be trusted to care for the interests of majorities. . . .

Democracy, however, though necessary, is by no means the only political condition required for the taming of power. It is possible, in a democracy, for the majority to exercise a brutal and wholly unnecessary tyranny over a minority. In the period from 1885 to 1922, the government of the United Kingdom was (except for the exclusion of women) democratic, but that did not prevent the oppression of Ireland. Not only a national, but a religious or political minority may be persecuted. The safeguarding of minorities, so far as is compatible with orderly government, is an essential part of the taming of power.

This requires a consideration of the matters as to which the community must act as a whole, and those as to which uniformity is unnecessary. The most obvious questions as to which a collective decision is imperative are those that are essentially geographical. Roads, railways, sewers, gas mains, and so on, must take one course and not another. Sanitary precautions, say against plague or rabies, are geographical: it would not do for Christian Scientists to announce that they will take no precautions against infection, because they might infect others. War is a geographical phenomenon, unless it is civil war, and even then it soon happens that one area is dominated by one side, and another by the other.

Where there is a geographically concentrated minority, such as the Irish before 1922, it is possible to solve a great many problems by devolution. But when the minority is distributed throughout the area concerned, this method is largely inapplicable. Where Christian and Mohammedan populations live side by side, they have, it is true, different marriage laws, but except where religion is concerned they all have to submit to one government. It has been gradually discovered that theological uniformity is not necessary to a State, and that Protestants and Catholics can live peaceably together under one government. But this was not the case during the first 130 years after the Reformation.

The question of the degree of liberty that is compatible with order is one that cannot be settled in the abstract. The only thing that can be said in the abstract is that, where there is no technical reason for a collective decision, there should be some strong reason connected with public order if freedom is to be interfered with. In the reign of Elizabeth, when Roman Catholics wished to deprive her of the throne, it is not surprising that the government viewed them with disfavour. Similarly in the Low Countries, where Protestants were in revolt against Spain, it was to be expected that the Spaniards would persecute them. Nowadays theological questions have not the same political importance. Even political differences, if they do not go too deep, are no reason for persecution. Conservatives, Liberals, and Labour people can all live peaceably side by side, because they do not wish to alter the Constitution by force; but Fascists and Communists are more difficult to assimilate. Where there is democracy, attempts of a minority to seize power by force, and incitements to such attempts, may reasonably be forbidden, on the ground that a law-abiding majority has a right to a quiet life if it can secure it. But there should be toleration of all propaganda not involving incitement to break the law, and the law should be as tolerant as is compatible with technical efficiency and the maintenance of order. . . .

From the point of view of the taming of power, very difficult questions arise as to the best size of a governmental unit. In a great modern State, even when it is a democracy, the ordinary citizen has very little sense of political power; he does not decide what are to be the issues in an election, they probably concern matters remote from his daily life and almost wholly outside his experience, and his vote makes so small a contribution to the total as to seem to himself negligible. In the ancient City State these evils were much less; so they are, at present, in local government. It might have been expected that the public would take more interest in local than in national questions, but this is not the case; on the contrary, the larger the area concerned, the greater is the percentage of the electorate that takes the trouble to vote. This is partly because more money is spent on propaganda in important elections, partly because the issues are in themselves more exciting. The most exciting issues are those involving war and relations to possible enemies. I remember an old yokel in January 1910, who told me he was going to vote Conservative (which was against his economic interests), because he had been persuaded that if the Liberals were victorious the Germans would be in the country within a week. It is not to be supposed that he ever voted in Parish Council elections, though in them he might have had some understanding of the issues; these issues failed to move him because they were not such as to generate mass hysteria or the myths upon which it feeds.

There is thus a dilemma: democracy gives a man a feeling that he has an effective share in political power when the group concerned is small, but not when it is large; on the other hand, the issue is likely to strike him as important when the group concerned is large, but not when it is small.

To some extent this difficulty is avoided when a constituency is vocational, not geographical; a really effective democracy is possible, for example, in a trade union. Each branch can meet to discuss a vexed question of policy; the members have a similarity of interest and experience, and this makes fruitful discussion possible. The final decision of the whole union may, therefore, be one in which a large percentage of members feel they have had a part.

This method, however, has obvious limitations. Many questions are so essentially geographical that a geographical constituency is unavoidable. Public bodies affect our lives at so many points that a busy man who is not a politician cannot take action about most of the local or national issues that concern him. The best solution would probably be an extension of the method of the trade union official, who is elected to represent a certain interest. At present, many interests have no such representative. Democracy, if it is to exist psychologically as well as politically, demands organisation of the various interests, and their representation, in political bargaining, by men who enjoy whatever influence is justified by the numbers and enthusiasm of their constituents. I do not mean that these representatives should be a substitute for Parliament, but that they should be the channel by which Parliament is made aware of the wishes of various groups of citizens....

II

I come now to the economic conditions required in order to minimise arbitrary power. This subject is of great importance, both on its own account, and because there has been a very great deal of confusion of thought in relation to it.

Political democracy, while it solves a part of our problem, does not by any means solve the whole. Marx pointed out that there could be no real equalisation of power through politics alone, while economic power remained monarchical or oligarchic. It followed that economic power must be in the hands of the State, and that the State must be democratic. Those who profess, at the present day, to be Marx's followers, have kept only the half of his doctrine, and have thrown over the demand that the State should be democratic. They have thus concentrated both economic and political power in the hands of an oligarchy, which has become, in consequence, more powerful and more able to exercise tyranny than any oligarchy of former times.

Both old-fashioned democracy and new-fashioned Marxism have aimed at the taming of power. The former failed because it was only political, the latter because it was only economic. Without a combination of both, nothing approaching to a solution of the problem is possible.

The arguments in favour of State ownership of land and the large economic organisations are partly technical, partly political. The technical arguments have not been much stressed except by the Fabian Society, and to some extent in America in connection with such matters as the Tennessee Valley Authority. Nevertheless they are very strong, especially in connection with electricity and water power, and cause even Conservative governments to introduce measures which, from a technical point of view, are socialistic. We have seen how, as a result of modern technique, organisations tend to grow and to coalesce and to increase their scope; the inevitable consequence is that the political State must either increasingly take over economic functions, or partially abdicate in favour of vast private enterprises which are sufficiently powerful to defy or control it. If the State does not acquire supremacy over such enterprises, it becomes their puppet, and they become the real State. In one way or another, wherever modern technique exists, economic and political power must become unified. This movement towards unification has the irresistible impersonal character which Marx attributed to the development that he prophesied. But it has nothing to do with the class war or the wrongs of the proletariat.

Socialism as a political movement has aimed at furthering the interests of industrial wage-earners; its technical advantages have been kept comparatively in the background. The belief is that the economic power of the private capitalist enables him to oppress the wage-earner, and that, since the wage-earner cannot, like the handicraftsman of former times, individually own his means of production, the only way of emanicipating him is collective ownership by the whole body of workers. It is argued that, if the private capitalist were expropriated, the whole body of the workers would constitute the State; and that, consequently, the problem of economic power can be solved completely by State ownership of land and capital, and in no other way. This is a proposal for the taming of economic power, and therefore comes within the purview of our present discussion.

Before examining the argument, I wish to say unequivocally that I consider it valid, provided it is adequately safeguarded and amplified. *Per contra*, in the absence of such safeguarding and amplifying I consider it very dangerous, and likely to mislead those who seek liberation from economic tyranny so completely that they will find they have inadvertently established a new tyranny at once economic and political, more drastic and more terrible than any previously known.

In the first place, 'ownership' is not the same thing as 'control'. If (say) a railway is owned by the State, and the State is considered to be the whole body of the citizens, that does not insure, of itself, that the average citizen will have any power over the railway. Let us revert, for a moment, to what Messrs Berle and Means say about ownership and control in large American corporations. They point out that, in the majority of such corporations, all the directors together usually own only about 1 or 2 per cent of the stock, and yet, in effect, have complete control:

> In the election of the board the stock holder ordinarily has three alternatives. He can refrain from voting, he can attend the annual meeting and personally vote his stock, or he can sign a proxy transferring his voting power to certain individuals selected by the management of the corporation, the proxy committee. As his personal vote will count for little or nothing at the meeting unless he has a very large block of stock, the stock holder is practically reduced to the alternative of not voting at all or else of *handing over his vote to individuals over whom he has no control and in whose selection he did not participate*. In neither case will he be able to exercise any measure of control. Rather, control will tend to be in the hands of those who select the proxy committee. . . . Since the proxy committee is appointed by the existing management, the latter can virtually dictate their own successors.[2]

[2] Berle and Means, *The Modern Corporation and Private Property* (Harcourt, Brace 1969), pp. 86–7.

The helpless individuals described in the above passage are, it should be noted, not proletarians, but capitalists. They are part owners of the corporation concerned, in the sense that they have legal rights which may, with luck, bring them in a certain income; but owing to their lack of control, the income is very precarious. . . .

The situation is in no way essentially different when the State takes the place of a corporation; indeed, since it is the size of the corporation that causes the helplessness of the average shareholder, the average citizen is likely to be still more helpless as against the State. A battleship is public property, but if, on this ground, you try to exercise rights of ownership, you will soon be put in your place. You have a remedy, it is true: at the next General Election, you can vote for a candidate who favours a reduction in the Navy Estimates, if you can find one; or you can write to the papers to urge that sailors should be more polite to sightseers. But more than this you cannot do.

But, it is said, the battleship belongs to a capitalist State, and when it belongs to a workers' State everything will be different. This view seems to me to show a failure to grasp the fact that economic power is now a matter of government rather than owner-ship. If the United States Steel Corporation, say, were taken over by the United States Government, it would still need men to manage it; they would either be the same men who now manage it, or men with similar abilities and a similar outlook. The attitude which they now have towards the shareholders they would then have towards the citizens. True, they would be subject to the government, but unless it was democratic and responsible to public opinion, it would have a point of view closely similar to that of the officials.

Marxists, having retained, as a result of the authority of Marx and Engels, many ways of thinking that belong to the forties of the last century, still conceive of businesses as if they belonged to individual capitalists, and have not learnt the lessons to be derived from the separation of ownership and control. The important person is the man who has control of economic power, not the man who has a fraction of the nominal ownership. The Prime Minister does not own No. 10 Downing Street, and Bishops do not own their palaces; but it would be absurd to pretend, on this account, that they are no better off as regards housing than the average wage-earner. Under any form of socialism which is not democratic, those who control economic power can, without 'owning' anything, have palatial official residences, the use of the best cars, a princely entertainment allowance, holidays at the public expense in official holiday resorts, and so on and so on. And why should they have any more concern for the ordinary worker than those in control have now? There can be no reason why they should have, unless the ordinary worker has power to deprive them of their positions. Moreover the subordination of the small investor in existing large corporations shows how easy it is for the official to overpower the democracy, even when the 'democracy' consists of capitalists.

Not only, therefore, is democracy essential if State ownership and control of economic enterprises is to be in any degree advantageous to the average citizen, but it will have to be an effective democracy, and this will be more difficult to secure than it is at present, since the official class will, unless very carefully supervised, combine the powers at present possessed by the government and the men in control of industry and finance, and since the means of agitating against the government will have to be supplied by the government itself, as the sole owner of halls, paper, and all the other essentials of propaganda.

While, therefore, public ownership and control of all large-scale industry and finance is a *necessary* condition for the taming of power, it is far from being a *sufficient* condition. It needs to be supplemented by a democracy more thorough-going, more carefully safeguarded against official tyranny, and with more deliberate provision for freedom of propaganda, than any purely political democracy that has ever existed.

Chapter 3

Democracy and Scientific Technique[1]

The word 'democracy' has become ambiguous. East of the Elbe it means 'military dictatorship of a minority enforced by arbitrary police power'. West of the Elbe its meaning is less definite, but broadly speaking it means 'even distribution of ultimate political power among all adults except lunatics, criminals and peers'. This is not a precise definition, because of the word 'ultimate'. Suppose the British Constitution were to be changed in only one respect: that General Elections should occur once in thirty years instead of once in five. This would so much diminish the dependence of Parliament on public opinion that the resulting system could hardly be called a democracy. Many Socialists would add economic to political power, as what demands even distribution in a democracy. But we may ignore these verbal questions. The essence of the matter is approach to equality of power, and it is obvious that democracy is a matter of degree.

When people think of democracy, they generally couple with it a considerable measure of liberty for individuals and groups. Religious persecution, for instance, would be excluded in imagination, although it is entirely compatible with democracy as defined a moment ago. I incline to think that 'liberty', as the word was understood in the eighteenth and nineteenth centuries, is no longer quite the right concept; I should prefer to substitute 'opportunity for initiative'. And my reason for suggesting this change is the character of a scientific society.

It cannot be denied that democracy no longer inspires the same enthusiasm as it inspired in Rousseau and the men of the French Revolution. This is, of course, mainly because it has been achieved. Advocates of a reform always overstate their case, so that their converts expect the reform to bring the millennium. When it fails to do so there is disappointment, even if very solid advantages are secured. In France under Louis XVI many people thought

[1] From *The Impact of Science on Society* (1952), pp. 55–7, 58–63, 65–6.

that all evils proceeded from kings and priests, so they cut off the king's head and turned priests into hunted fugitives. But still they failed to enjoy celestial bliss. So they decided that although kings are bad there is no harm in emperors.

So it has been with democracy. Its sober advocates, notably Bentham, and his school, maintained that it would do away with certain evils, and on the whole they proved right. But its enthusiasts, the followers of Rousseau especially, thought that it could achieve far more than there was good reason to expect. Its sober successes were forgotten, just because the evils which it had cured were no longer there to cause indignation. Consequently people listened to Carlyle's ridicule and Nietzsche's savage invective against it as the ethic of slaves. In many minds the cult of the hero replaced the cult of the common man. And the cult of the hero, in practice, is Fascism.

The cult of the hero is anarchic and retrograde, and does not easily fit in with the needs of a scientific society. But there is an opposite tendency, embodied in communism, which, though also anti-democratic, is in line with the technical developments of modern industry, and therefore much more worthy of consideration. This is the tendency to attach importance neither to heroes nor to common men, but to organisations. In this view the individual is nothing apart from the social bodies of which he is a member. Each such body – so it is said – represents some social force, and it is only as part of such a force that an individual is of importance.

We have thus three points of view, leading to three different political philosophies. You may view an individual (*a*) as a common man, (*b*) as a hero, (*c*) as a cog in the machine. The first view leads you to old-fashioned democracy, the second to fascism, and the third to communism. I think that democracy, if it is to recover the power of inspiring vigorous action, needs to take account of what is valid in the other two ways of regarding individuals.

Everybody exemplifies all three points of view in different situations. Even if you are the greatest of living poets, you are a common man where your ration book is concerned, or when you go to the polling booth to vote. However humdrum your daily life may be, there is a good chance that you will now and again have an opportunity for heroism: you may save someone from drowning, or (more likely) you may die nobly in battle. You are a cog in the machine if you work in an organised group, for example, the army or the mining industry. What science has done is to increase the proportion of your life in which you are a cog, to the extent of endangering what is due to you as a hero or as a common man. The business of a modern advocate of democracy is to develop a political philosophy which avoids this danger.

In a good social system, every man will be at once a hero, a common man, and a cog, to the greatest possible extent, though if he is any one of these in an exceptional degree his other two roles may be diminished. *Qua* hero, a man should have the opportunity of initiative; *qua* common man, he should have security; *qua* cog, he should be useful. A nation cannot achieve great excellence by any one of these alone. In Poland before the partition, all were heroes (at least all nobles); the Middle West is the home of the common man; and in Russia everyone outside the Politburo is a cog. No one of these three is quite satisfactory. . . .

The main point is this: scientific technique, by making society more organic, increases the extent to which an individual is a cog; if this is not to be an evil, ways must be found of preventing him from being a *mere* cog. This means that initiative must be preserved in spite of organisation. But most initiative will be what may be called in a large sense 'political', that is to say, it will consist of advice as to what some organisation should do. And if there is to be opportunity for this sort of initiative, organisations must, as far as possible, be governed democratically. Not only so, but the federal principle must be carried so far that every energetic person can hope to influence the government of *some* social group of which he is a member.

Democracy, at present, defeats its object by the vastness of the constituencies involved. Suppose you are an American, interested in a Presidential election. If you are a Senator or a Congressman, you can have a considerable influence, but the odds are about 100,000 to 1 that you are neither. If you are a ward politician you can do something. But if you are an ordinary citizen you can only vote. And I do not think there has ever been a Presidential election where one man's abstention would have altered the result. And so you feel as powerless as if you lived under a dictatorship. You are, of course, committing the classical fallacy of the heap, but most people's minds work that way.

In England is it not quite so bad, because there is no election in which the whole nation is one constituency. In 1945 I worked for a candidate who got a majority of forty-six, so if my work converted twenty-four people the result would have been different if I had been idle. If the Labour Party had got a majority of one in Parliament I might have come to think myself quite important; but as it was I had to content myself with the pleasure of being on the winning side.

Things would be better if people took an interest in local politics, but unfortunately few do. Nor is this surprising, since most of the important issues are decided nationally, not locally. It is to be regretted that there is so little civic pride nowadays. In the middle ages each city wished to be pre-eminent in the splendour of its cathedral, and we still profit by the result. In our own time, Stockholm had the same feeling about its Town Hall, which is splendid. But English large towns seem to have no such feeling.

In industry there is room for a great deal of devolution. For many years the Labour Party has advocated nationalisation of railways, and most railway employees have supported the Party in this. But now a good many of them are finding that the State is, after all, not so very different from a private company. It is equally remote, and under a Conservative government it will be equally likely to be on bad terms with the unions. In fact nationalisation needs to be supplemented by a measure of limited self-government for the railways, the railway government being elected democratically by the employees.

In all federal systems, the general principle should be to divide the affairs of each component body into home affairs and foreign affairs, the component bodies having free control of their home affairs, and the federal body having authority in matters which are foreign affairs for the components but not for it. It, in turn, should be a unit in a wider federation, and so on until we reach the World Government, which, for the present, would have no foreign affairs. Of course it is not always easy to decide whether a matter is purely local or not, but this will be a question for the law courts, as in America and Australia.

This principle should be applied not only geographically, but also vocationally. In old days, when travel was slow and roads often impassable, geographical location was more important than it is now. Now, especially in a small country like ours, there would be no difficulty in allocating certain governmental functions to bodies like the trade unions, which classify people by their occupation, not by their habitation. The foreign relations of an industry are access to raw material, quantity and price of finished product. These it should not control. But everything else it should be free to decide for itself.

In such a system, there would be many more opportunities of individual initiative than there are at present, although central control would remain wherever it is essential. Of course the system would be difficult to work in time of war, and so long as there is imminent risk of war it is impossible to escape from the authority of the State except to a very limited degree. It is mainly war that has caused the excessive power of modern States, and until the fear of war is removed it is inevitable that everything should be subordinated to short-term efficiency. But I have thought it worth while to think for a moment of the world as it may be when a World Government has ended the present nightmare dread of war.

In addition to the kind of federalism that I have been speaking of, there is, for certain purposes, a somewhat different method which can be advantageous. It is that of bodies which, though really part of the State, have a very considerable degree of independence. Such are, for example, the universities, the Royal Society, the BBC, and the Port of London Authority. The smooth working of such bodies depends upon a certain degree of homogeneity in the community. If the Royal Society or the BBC came to contain a majority of Communists, Parliament would no doubt curtail its liberties. But in the meantime both have a good deal of autonomy, which is highly desirable. Our older universities, being governed by men with a respect for learning, are, I am happy to observe, much more liberal towards academically distinguished Communists than the universities of America, in which men of learning have no voice in the government.

Art and literature are peculiar in the modern world in that those who practise them retain the individual liberty of former times, and are practically untouched by scientific technique unless they are drawn into the cinema. This is more true of authors than of artists, because, as private fortunes dwindle, artists become increasingly dependent upon the patronage of public bodies. But if an artist is prepared to starve, nothing can prevent him from doing his best. However, the position of both artists and authors is precarious. In Russia they are already mere licensed sycophants.

Elsewhere, before long, with conscription of labour, no one will be allowed to practise literature or painting unless he can get twelve magistrates or ministers of religion to testify to his competence. I am not quite sure that the aesthetic taste of these worthy men will always be impeccable.

Liberty, in the old-fashioned sense, is much more important in regard to mental than to material goods. The reason is simple: that in regard to mental goods what one man possesses is not taken from other men, whereas with material goods it is otherwise. When a limited supply of (say) food has to be shared out, the obvious principle is *justice*. This does not mean exact equality: a navvy needs more food than a bed-ridden old man. The principle must be, in the words of the old slogan, 'to each according to his needs'. There is here, however, a difficulty, much emphasised by opponents of Socialism; it is that of incentive. Under capitalism, the incentive is fear of starvation; under communism, it is the fear of drastic police punishment. Neither is quite what the democratic socialist wants. But I do not think industry can work efficiently through the mere motive of public spirit; something more personal is necessary in normal times. My own belief is that a collective profit motive can be, and should be, combined with Socialism. Take, say, coalmining. The State should decide, at the beginning of each year, what prices it is prepared to pay for coal of various qualities. Methods of mining should be left to the industry. Every technical improvement would then result in more coal or less work for miners. The profit motive, in a new form, would survive, but without the old evils. By devolution, the motive could be made to operate on each mine.

In regard to mental goods, neither justice nor incentive is important; what is important is *opportunity*. Opportunity, of course, includes remaining alive, and to this extent involves material goods. But most men of great creative power are not interested in becoming rich, so that a modest subsistence would suffice. And if these men are put to death, like Socrates, when their work is done, no harm is done to anyone. But great harm is done if, during their lifetime, their work is hampered by authority, even if the hampering takes the form of heaping honours upon them as the price of conformity. No society can be progressive without a leaven of rebels, and modern technique makes it more and more difficult to be a rebel.

The difficulties of this problem are very great. As regards science, I do not think that any complete solution is possible. You cannot

work at nuclear physics in America unless you are politically orthodox; you cannot work at any science in Russia unless you are
orthodox, not only in politics, but also in science, and orthodoxy
in science means accepting all Stalin's uneducated prejudices. The
difficulty arises from the vast expense of scientific apparatus. There
is, or was, a law that when a man is sued for debt he must not be
deprived of the tools of his trade, but when his tools cost many
millions of pounds the situation is very different from that of the
eighteenth-century handicraftsman.

I do not think that, in the present state of the world, any government can be blamed for demanding *political* orthodoxy of nuclear
physicists. If Guy Fawkes had demanded gunpowder on the ground
that it was one of the tools of his trade, I think James I's government would have viewed the request somewhat coldly, and this
applies with even more force to the nuclear physicists of our time:
governments must demand some assurance as to who they are
going to blow up. But there is no justification whatever for demanding *scientific* orthodoxy. Fortunately in science it is fairly easy to
estimate a man's ability. It is therefore possible to act on the principle
that a scientist should be given opportunity in proportion to his
ability, not to his scientific orthodoxy. I think that on the whole,
in Western Europe, this principle is fairly well observed. But its
observance is precarious, and might easily cease in a time of acute
scientific controversy.

In art and literature the problem is different. On the one hand,
freedom is more possible, because the authorities are not asked to
provide expensive apparatus. But on the other hand merit is much
more difficult to estimate. The older generation of artists and
writers is almost invariably mistaken as to the younger generation:
the pundits almost always condemn the new men who are subsequently judged to have outstanding merit. For this reason such
bodies as the French Academy or the Royal Academy are useless,
if not harmful. There is no conceivable method by which the
community can recognise the artist until he is old and most of his
work is done. The community can only give opportunity and
toleration. It can hardly be expected that the community should
license every man who says he means to paint, and should support
him for his daubs however execrable they may be. I think the
only solution is that the artist should support himself by work
other than his art, until such time as he gets a knighthood. He should

seek ill-paid half-time employment, live austerely, and do his creative work in his spare time. Sometimes less arduous solutions are possible: a dramatist can be an actor, a composer can be a performer. But in any case the artist or writer must, while he is young, keep his creative work outside the economic machine and make his living by work of which the value is obvious to the authorities. For if his creative work affords his official means of livelihood, it will be hampered and impaired by the ignorant censorship of the authorities. The most that can be hoped – and this is much – is that a man who does good work will not be punished for it. . . .

A democratic scientific society, by exacting service and conferring security, forbids or prevents much personal initiative which is possible in a less well-regulated world. Eighty years ago, Vanderbilt and Jay Gould each claimed ownership of the Erie Railroad; each had a printing press to prove how many shares he owned; each had a posse of corrupt judges ready to give any legal decision demanded of them; each had physical control of a portion of the rolling stock. On a given day, one started a train at one end of the line, the other at the other; the trains met in the middle; each was full of hired bravos, and the two gangs had a six-hour battle. Obviously Vanderbilt and Jay Gould enjoyed themselves hugely; so did the bravos; so did the whole American nation except those who wanted to use the Erie Railroad. So did I when I read about the affair. Nevertheless, the affair was thought to be a scandal. Nowadays the impulse to such delights has to seek satisfaction in the construction of hydrogen bombs, which is at once more harmful and less emotionally satisfying. If the world is ever to have peace, it must find ways of combining peace with the possibility of adventures that are not destructive.

The solution lies in providing opportunities for contests that are not conducted by violent means. This is one of the great merits of democracy. If you hate socialism or capitalism, you are not reduced to assassinating Mr Attlee or Mr Churchill; you can make election speeches, or, if that doesn't satisfy you, get yourself elected to Parliament. So long as the old Liberal freedoms survive, you can engage in propaganda for whatever excites you. Such activities suffice to satisfy most men's combative instincts. Creative impulses which are not combative, such as those of the artist and the writer, cannot be satisfied in this way, and for them the only solution, in a Socialist state, is liberty to employ your leisure as you like. This is the only solution, because such activities are sometimes extremely valuable, but the community has no way of judging, in a given case, whether the artist's or writer's work is worthless or shows immortal genius. Such activities, therefore, must not be systematised or controlled. Some part of life – perhaps the most important part – must be left to the spontaneous action of individual impulse, for where all is system there will be mental and spiritual death.

Further Readings

RUSSELL

'The State' in *Principles of Social Reconstruction*
'Property' in *Principles of Social Reconstruction*
'Government and Law' in *Roads to Freedom*
'The Individual versus the Citizen' in *Education and the Social Order*
'The Reconciliation of Individuality and Citizenship' in *Education and the Social Order*
'The Case for Socialism' in *In Praise of Idleness*
'Freedom in Society' in *Sceptical Essays*
'Freedom versus Authority in Education' in *Sceptical Essays*
'Free Thought and Official Propaganda' in *Sceptical Essays*
'Control and Initiative' in *Authority and the Individual*

OTHER AUTHORS

Berlin, I., *Two Concepts of Liberty* (Oxford University Press 1958)
Coates, K. and Topham, T. (eds), *Workers' Control* (Panther 1970)
Glass, S. T., *The Responsible Society: The Ideas of Guild Socialism* (Longmans 1966)
Mill, J. S., *On Liberty* (1859; available in many editions)
Vaizey, J., *Social Democracy* (Weidenfeld & Nicolson 1971)

Part Two

Religion

Introduction

RUSSELL'S RATIONAL SCEPTICISM

'My own view of religion,' writes Russell, 'is that of Lucretius. I regard it as a disease born of fear and as a source of untold misery to the human race.'[1] Russell's opinion is an uncompromising one, but not one to be rejected without a sincere attempt to meet his arguments. These arguments many have found compelling – indeed, we see in our time much debate between Christians and unbelievers on the claims of Christianity and on its supposed moral and social benefits. The Churches have not always been so ready to listen to criticism levelled against their dogma, preferring when political power was available to use such methods as are even now present in totalitarian states for countering unorthodoxy.

The general intellectual position Russell adopts is one of 'rational scepticism', the simple and apparently admirable one of not taking something as certain where evidence is insufficient. This kind of scepticism is very well expressed in his Liberal Decalogue (Chapter 4 below), and the great force of his arguments against Christianity becomes clear as we realise that most of Russell's Ten Commandments have indeed been broken by it. The Decalogue represents one of Russell's central objections to Christianity, and to religion in general, for it is diametrically opposed to any *creed*, or *dogma*, any set of beliefs which are adhered to in the face of an obvious lack of evidence to support them.

THE OBJECTIONS TO DOGMA

Russell's objections to dogma can usefully be divided into the *intellectual* and the *moral*. The *intellectual* objection is directed at the insistence that various doubtful propositions are known to be true. For example, the proposition that there is a life after death is not known to be true, and on this question suspension of judgement is the only rational attitude; the claim that there is a future

---

[1] 'Has Religion Made Useful Contributions to Civilisation?', p. 28. (For full references to this and other papers mentioned see the list of Further Readings on p. 85.)

life may be true, but the very different claim that it is certainly true is not. (See 'Religion in Education' for a fuller discussion of this line of attack.) The *moral* objections to dogma are numerous, and one of the most telling which Russell raises is that an insistence on dogmatic claims inhibits social changes which are essential for the happiness of mankind. What this comes to is not so much that present creeds are greatly responsible for the miseries of human existence (though, as we shall see below, Russell believes that to be true also), but rather that the opposite attitude of rational scepticism is a condition of the emergence of a happier and more harmonious society: only by the free use of intelligence, unencumbered by any creed, can we discover and initiate the way to individual and social well-being. (This theme is followed up in 'On the Value of Scepticism' and 'Can Religion Cure our Troubles?'.) A second moral argument against dogma concerns the ever present danger of the enforcement of official creeds, with the discouragement of inquiry and other attendant evils: 'Positions of authority will be open to the orthodox. Historical records must be falsified if they throw doubt on received opinions. Sooner or later unorthodoxy will come to be considered a crime to be dealt with by the stake, the purge, or the concentration camp'.[2]

So far, Russell's arguments have been directed against any dogmatic principles as such, any creed of a religion or political organisation. In the selections reprinted here Russell is concerned primarily with a detailed consideration of dogmas peculiar to Christianity, and in the following sketch of his position it will be useful again to distinguish between intellectual and moral objections.

INTELLECTUAL OBJECTIONS TO CHRISTIANITY

Chapter 5 below contains Russell's criticism of the central doctrine of Christianity, namely the existence of God. (He also discusses, in passing, the doctrine of the immortality of the soul, though a much fuller discussion of this doctrine can be found in 'Do We Survive Death?'.) I will set out very briefly the arguments for God's existence which Russell is concerned to refute, with an indication of his line of attack.

1. *The First Cause Argument*. This goes as follows: everything

[2] 'Can Religion Cure our Troubles?', p. 162.

in this world has a cause which precedes it; there must be a beginning of this causal sequence, a 'First Cause'; *ergo* God, the First Cause, exists. In reply, Russell points out quite simply that even if the premiss of this argument is accepted, the beginning of the sequence may as well be the world as God.

2. *The Natural Law Argument*: there are laws of nature; a law of nature implies a lawgiver; *ergo* God, the lawgiver, exists. Russell rejects this conclusion on the grounds that 'natural laws', not being commands to behave in certain ways but simply descriptions of the ways things do in fact behave, do not imply a lawgiver.

3. *The Argument from Design*: the world exhibits purpose in its construction; *ergo* there must be a God who so designed it. Russell's reply is that whatever 'design' there is in the world, for example the way living creatures are peculiarly suited to their environment, may be explained just as well in other terms, such as natural selection.

4. *The Moral Argument* (supposed by Russell to originate from Kant): some things are morally right and others wrong; this could not be so unless God existed; *ergo* God exists. Russell asks why the distinction between right and wrong is thought to rest on God's existence – for if (as is apparently the case) the suggestion is that an act is wrong because God so wills it, then nothing would be right or wrong independently of God's will, and the undesirable consequences follow that there is no right and wrong for God and that 'God is good' is an insignificant statement.

5. *The Argument from the Remedying of Injustice*: there is much injustice in the world we inhabit; there must be a future life to redress the balance; *ergo* God exists, and so do heaven, hell and eternal damnation. Russell's reply is that the existence of injustice as much affords an argument *against* the existence of a benevolent deity.

MORAL OBJECTIONS TO CHRISTIANITY

Here Russell's arguments concern the moral failing of the Churches both in the doctrines they have preached and in the influence they have exerted throughout their history. In the section on Christian Ethics (Chapter 6), he argues that the Christian view of marriage, epitomised in St Paul's statement that it is better to marry than to burn, is responsible for 'mental disorders and unwholesome views of life'; and he raises the question of the degree of blame to be apportioned to Christian doctrine for the subjection of women. He also makes out a case against the supposed moral perfection of Christ (Chapter 5), questioning the morality contained in, and social desirability of, a doctrine of sin and damnation. And, of course, the history of Christianity has left much to be desired:

> Christianity has been distinguished from other religions by its greater readiness for persecution. . . . Anti-Semitism was promoted by Christianity from the moment when the Roman Empire became Christian. The religious fervour of the Crusades led to pogroms in Western Europe. It was Christians who unjustly accused Dreyfus, and free-thinkers who secured his final rehabilitation. . . . The abominations of King Leopold's government of the Congo were concealed or minimised by the Church and were ended only by an agitation conducted mainly by free-thinkers.[3]

COMMENTS

Russell's case against religion in general, and Christianity in particular, is many-sided and apparently very strong – it presents the Christian with an unenviable task of defence. One or two lines that might be tried are as follows:

Christian dogma. It might be said that, though Russell is right to denounce dogma in general, at least the Christian dogmas with their emphasis on love and the brotherhood of man have been and continue to be a force for good. But (1) is this so? (Russell has produced a case against it), and (2) whatever good has resulted from these dogmas has to be weighed against the evils attending their enforcement.

Moral objections to Christianity. The Christian might want to distinguish between Christianity itself and the Churches, and go on to argue that the unfortunate cruel face of Christianity exhibited in the history of persecution and intolerance is not a true reflection of its essential teachings – 'they were not true Christians'. Yet how far is Christian doctrine itself removed from the taint of persecu-

---

[3] 'Can Religion Cure our Troubles?', p. 166. See also 'Religion and the Churches'.

tion and intolerance, encompassing as it does such ideas as sin, damnation, and the wickedness of unbelievers?

Intellectual objections to Christianity. It could be said that Russell's exposition of the various arguments for God's existence are only parodies of these arguments as actually used. This is certainly true of the Moral Argument, if it is supposed to represent what Kant had in mind; whether it is generally true can be discovered only by examining the things Christians actually say – see, for example, the debate between Russell and Copleston on 'The Existence of God'. However, even without such an examination, we can ask whether Russell has succeeded in refuting the arguments as he represents them, and it does look as though Christians could meet some of his attacks. For example, in defending the Moral Argument the Christian need not deny the conclusion Russell draws, that 'God is good' lacks a meaning: alternatively, he could say that 'good' signifies something different when applied to God from what it signifies when applied to the actions of His subjects – both these replies would undermine Russell's argument.

QUESTIONS

1. If the Churches hold certain dogma as articles of faith, how can they think that arguments are available to support them?

2. Consider carefully Russell's reasons for rejecting the traditional arguments for God's existence. Try to present a defence of these arguments.

3. Was Jesus Christ a good Christian?

4. In your opinion, has Russell succeeded in showing that Christianity has been, on the whole, a force for evil?

5. If modern Christian doctrine rejects the idea of hell and damnation, can it continue to accept the idea of heaven?

Chapter 4

A Liberal Decalogue[1]

Perhaps the essence of the Liberal outlook could be summed up in a new decalogue, not intended to replace the old one but only to supplement it. The Ten Commandments that, as a teacher, I should wish to promulgate, might be set forth as follows:

1. Do not feel absolutely certain of anything.
2. Do not think it worth while to proceed by concealing evidence, for the evidence is sure to come to light.
3. Never try to discourage thinking for you are sure to succeed.
4. When you meet with opposition . . . endeavour to overcome it by argument and not by authority, for a victory dependent upon authority is unreal and illusory.
5. Have no respect for the authority of others, for there are always contrary authorities to be found.
6. Do not use power to suppress opinions you think pernicious, for if you do the opinions will suppress you.
7. Do not fear to be eccentric in opinion, for every opinion now accepted was once eccentric.
8. Find more pleasure in intelligent dissent than in passive agreement, for, if you value intelligence as you should, the former implies a deeper agreement than the latter.
9. Be scrupulously truthful, even if the truth is inconvenient, for it is more inconvenient when you try to conceal it.
10. Do not feel envious of the happiness of those who live in a fool's paradise, for only a fool will think that it is happiness.

[1] From *Autobiography of Bertrand Russell*, vol. iii, p. 60.

Chapter 5

Why I am Not a Christian[1]

There are two different items which are quite essential to anybody calling himself a Christian. The first is one of a dogmatic nature – namely, that you must believe in God and immortality. If you do not believe in those two things, I do not think that you can properly call yourself a Christian. Then, further than that, as the name implies, you must have some kind of belief about Christ. The Mohammedans, for instance, also believe in God and in immortality, and yet they would not call themselves Christians. I think you must have at the very lowest the belief that Christ was, if not divine, at least the best and wisest of men. If you are not going to believe that much about Christ, I do not think you have any right to call yourself a Christian. . . . Therefore I take it that when I tell you why I am not a Christian I have to tell you two different things; first, why I do not believe in God and in immortality; and, secondly, why I do not think that Christ was the best and wisest of men, although I grant Him a very high degree of moral goodness.

But for the successful efforts of unbelievers in the past, I could not take so elastic a definition of Christianity as that. . . . In olden days it had a much more full-blooded sense. For instance, it included the belief in hell. Belief in eternal hell fire was an essential item of Christian belief until pretty recent times. In this country, as you know, it ceased to be an essential item because of a decision of the Privy Council, and from that decision the Archbishop of Canterbury and the Archbishop of York dissented; but in this country our religion is settled by Act of Parliament, and therefore the Privy Council was able to override Their Graces and hell was no longer necessary to a Christian. Consequently I shall not insist that a Christian must believe in hell.

[1] From *Why I am Not a Christian* (1957), pp. 13–27. (Written in 1927.)

THE EXISTENCE OF GOD

To come to this question of the existence of God, it is a large and serious question, and if I were to attempt to deal with it in any adequate manner I should have to keep you here until Kingdom Come, so that you will have to excuse me if I deal with it in a somewhat summary fashion. You know, of course, that the Catholic Church has laid it down as a dogma that the existence of God can be proved by the unaided reason. That is a somewhat curious dogma, but it is one of their dogmas. They had to introduce it because at one time the Freethinkers adopted the habit of saying that there were such and such arguments which mere reason might urge against the existence of God, but of course they knew as a matter of faith that God did exist. The arguments and the reasons were set out at great length, and the Catholic Church felt that they must stop it. Therefore they laid it down that the existence of God can be proved by the unaided reason, and they had to set up what they considered were arguments to prove it. There are, of course, a number of them, but I shall take only a few.

THE FIRST CAUSE ARGUMENT

Perhaps the simplest and easiest to understand is the argument of the First Cause. (It is maintained that everything we see in this world has a cause, and as you go back in the chain of causes further and further you must come to a First Cause, and to that First Cause you give the name of God.) That argument, I suppose, does not carry very much weight nowadays, because, in the first place, cause is not quite what it used to be. The philosophers and the men of science have got going on cause, and it has not anything like the vitality it used to have; but, apart from that, you can see that the argument that there must be a First Cause is one that cannot have any validity. I may say that when I was a young man and was debating these questions very seriously in my mind, I for a long time accepted the argument of the First Cause, until one day, at the age of eighteen, I read John Stuart Mill's Autobiography, and I there found this sentence: 'My father taught me that the question, "Who made me?" cannot be answered, since it immediately suggests the further question, "Who made God?".' That very simple sentence showed me, as I still think, the fallacy in the argument of the

First Cause. If everything must have a cause, then God must have a cause. If there can be anything without a cause, it may just as well be the world as God, so that there cannot be any validity in that argument. It is exactly of the same nature as the Hindu's view, that the world rested upon an elephant and the elephant rested upon a tortoise; and when they said, 'How about the tortoise?' the Indian said, 'Suppose we change the subject.' The argument is really no better than that. There is no reason why the world could not have come into being without a cause; nor, on the other hand, is there any reason why it should not have always existed. There is no reason to suppose that the world had a beginning at all. The idea that things must have a beginning is really due to the poverty of our imagination. Therefore, perhaps, I need not waste any more time upon the argument about the First Cause.

THE NATURAL LAW ARGUMENT

Then there is a very common argument from natural law. That was a favourite argument all through the eighteenth century, especially under the influence of Sir Isaac Newton and his cosmogony. People observed the planets going round the sun according to the law of gravitation, and they thought that God had given a behest to these planets to move in that particular fashion, and that was why they did so. That was, of course, a convenient and simple explanation that saved them the trouble of looking any further for explanations of the law of gravitation. Nowadays we explain the law of gravitation in a somewhat complicated fashion that Einstein has introduced. I do not proposed to give you a lecture on the law of gravitation as interpreted by Einstein, because that again would take some time; at any rate, you no longer have the sort of natural law that you had in the Newtonian system, where, for some reason that nobody could understand, nature behaved in a uniform fashion. We now find that a great many things we thought were natural laws are really human conventions. You know that even in the remotest depths of stellar space there are still 3 feet to a yard. That is, no doubt, a very remarkable fact, but you would hardly call it a law of nature. And a great many things that have been regarded as laws of nature are of that kind. On the other hand, where you can get down to any knowledge of what atoms actually do, you will find they are much less subject to law than people thought, and that the laws at which you arrive are statistical averages of just the sort that would emerge from chance. There is, as we all know, a law that if you throw dice you will get double sixes only about once in thirty-six times, and we do not regard that as evidence that the fall of the dice is regulated by design; on the contrary, if the double sixes came every time we should think that there was design. The laws of nature are of that sort as regards a great many of them. They are statistical averages such as would emerge from the laws of chance; and that makes this whole business of natural law much less impressive than it formerly was. Quite apart from that, which represents the momentary state of science that may change tomorrow, the whole idea that natural laws imply a law-giver is due to a confusion between natural and human laws. Human laws are behests commanding you to behave a certain way, in which way you may choose to behave, or you may choose not to behave; but natural laws are a description of how things do in fact behave, and being a mere description of what they in fact do, you cannot argue that there must be somebody who told them to do that, because even supposing that there were you are then faced with the question, 'Why did God issue just those natural laws and no others?' If you say that He did it simply from His own good pleasure, and without any reason, you then find that there is something which is not subject to law, and so your train of natural laws is interrupted. If you say, as more orthodox theologians do, that in all the laws which God issues He had a reason for giving those laws rather than others – the reason, of course, being to create the best universe, although you would never think it to look at it – if there was a reason for the laws which God gave, then God Himself was subject to law, and therefore you do not get any advantage by introducing God as an intermediary. You have really a law outside and anterior to the divine edicts, and God does not serve your purpose, because He is not the ultimate law-giver. In short, this whole argument about natural law no longer has anything like the strength that it used to have. I am travelling on in time in my review of the arguments. The arguments that are used for the existence of God change their character as time goes on. They were at first hard, intellectual arguments embodying certain quite definite fallacies. As we come to modern times they become less respectable intellectually and more and more affected by a kind of moralising vagueness.

THE ARGUMENT FROM DESIGN

The next step in this process brings us to the argument from design. You all know the argument from design: everything in the world is made just so that we can manage to live in the world, and if the world was ever so little different we could not manage to live in it. That is the argument from design. It sometimes takes a rather curious form; for instance, it is argued that rabbits have white tails in order to be easy to shoot. I do not know how rabbits would view that application. It is an easy argument to parody. You all know Voltaire's remark, that obviously the nose was designed to be such as to fit spectacles. That sort of parody has turned out to be not nearly so wide of the mark as it might have seemed in the eighteenth century, because since the time of Darwin we understand much better why living creatures are adapted to their environment. It is not that their environment was made to be suitable to them, but that they grew to be suitable to it, and that is the basis of adaptation. There is no evidence of design about it.

When you come to look into this argument from design, it is a most astonishing thing that people can believe that this world, with all the things that are in it, with all its defects, should be the best that omnipotence and omniscience have been able to produce in millions of years. I really cannot believe it. Do you think that, if you were granted omnipotence and omniscience and millions of years in which to perfect your world, you could produce nothing better than the Ku-Klux-Klan or the Fascists? Moreover, if you accept the ordinary laws of science, you have to suppose that human life and life in general on this planet will die out in due course: it is a stage in the decay of the solar system; at a certain stage of decay you get the sort of conditions of temperature and so forth which are suitable to protoplasm, and there is life for a short time in the life of the whole solar system. You see in the moon the sort of thing to which the earth is tending – something dead, cold and lifeless.

I am told that that sort of view is depressing, and people will sometimes tell you that if they believed that they would not be able to go on living. Do not believe it; it is all nonsense. Nobody really worries much about what is going to happen millions of years hence. Even if they think they are worrying much about that, they are really deceiving themselves. They are worried about something much more mundane, or it may merely be a bad digestion; but nobody is really seriously rendered unhappy by the thought of something that is going to happen to this world millions of years hence. Therefore, although it is of course a gloomy view to suppose that life will die out – at least I suppose we may say so, although sometimes when I contemplate the things that people do with their lives I think it is almost a consolation – it is not such as to render life miserable. It merely makes you turn your attention to other things.

THE MORAL ARGUMENTS FOR DEITY

Now we reach one stage further in what I shall call the intellectual descent that the Theists have made in their argumentations, and we come to what are called the moral arguments for the existence of God. You all know, of course, that there used to be in the old days three intellectual arguments for the existence of God, all of which were disposed of by Immanuel Kant in the *Critique of Pure Reason*; but no sooner had he disposed of those arguments than he invented a new one, a moral argument, and that quite convinced him. He was like many people: in intellectual matters he was sceptical, but in moral matters he believed implicitly in the maxims that he had imbibed at his mother's knee. That illustrates what the psycho-analysts so much emphasise – the immensely stronger hold upon us that our very early associations have than those of later times.

Kant, as I say, invented a new moral argument for the existence of God, and that in varying forms was extremely popular during the nineteenth century. It has all sorts of forms. One form is to say that there would be no right or wrong unless God existed. I am not for the moment concerned with whether there is a difference between right and wrong, or whether there is not: that is another question. The point I am concerned with is that, if you are quite sure there is a difference between right and wrong, you are then in this situation: is that difference due to God's fiat or is it not? If it is due to God's fiat, then for God Himself there is no difference between right and wrong, and it is no longer a significant statement to say that God is good. If you are going to say, as theologians do, that God is good, you must then say that right and wrong have some meaning which is independent of God's fiat, because God's fiats are good and not bad independently of the mere fact that He made them. If you are going to say that, you will then have to say that it is not only through

God that right and wrong came into being, but that they are in their essence logically anterior to God. You could, of course, if you liked, say that there was a superior deity who gave orders to the God who made this world, or could take up the line that some of the gnostics took up – a line which I often thought was a very plausible one – that as a matter of fact this world that we know was made by the devil at a moment when God was not looking. There is a good deal to be said for that, and I am not concerned to refute it.

THE ARGUMENT FOR THE REMEDYING OF INJUSTICE

Then there is another very curious form of moral argument, which is this: they say that the existence of God is required in order to bring justice into the world. In the part of this universe that we know there is great injustice, and often the good suffer, and often the wicked prosper, and one hardly knows which of those is the more annoying; but if you are going to have justice in the universe as a whole you have to suppose a future life to redress the balance of life here on earth. So they say that there must be a God, and there must be heaven and hell in order that in the long run there may be justice. That is a very curious argument. If you looked at the matter from a scientific point of view, you would say: 'After all, I know only this world. I do not know about the rest of the universe, but so far as one can argue at all on probabilities one would say that probably this world is a fair sample, and if there is injustice here the odds are that there is injustice elsewhere also.' Supposing you got a crate of oranges that you opened, and you found all the top layer of oranges bad, you would not argue: 'The underneath ones must be good, so as to redress the balance.' You would say: 'Probably the whole lot is a bad consignment'; and that is really what a scientific person would argue about the universe. He would say: 'Here we find in this world a great deal of injustice and so far as that goes that is a reason for supposing that justice does not rule in the world; and therefore so far as it goes it affords a moral argument against deity and not in favour of one.' Of course I know that the sort of intellectual arguments that I have been talking to you about are not what really moves people. What really moves people to believe in God is not any intellectual arguments at all. Most people believe in God because they have been taught from early infancy to do it, and that is the main reason.

Then I think that the next most powerful reason is the wish for safety, a sort of feeling that there is a big brother who will look after you. That plays a very profound part in influencing people's desire for a belief in God.

THE CHARACTER OF CHRIST

I now want to say a few words upon a topic which I often think is not quite sufficiently dealt with by Rationalists, and that is the question whether Christ was the best and the wisest of men. It is generally taken for granted that we should all agree that that was so. I do not myself. I think that there are a good many points upon which I agree with Christ a great deal more than the professing Christians do. I do not know that I could go with Him all the way, but I could go with Him much further than most professing Christians can. You will remember that He said: 'Resist not evil, but whosoever shall smite thee on thy right cheek, turn to him the other also.' That is not a new precept or a new principle. It was used by Lao-tze and Buddha some five or six hundred years before Christ, but it is not a principle which as a matter of fact Christians accept. I have no doubt that the present Prime Minister,[2] for instance, is a most sincere Christian, but I should not advise any of you to go and smite him on one cheek. I think you might find that he thought this text was intended in a figurative sense.

Then there is another point which I consider is excellent. You will remember that Christ said: 'Judge not lest ye be judged.' That principle I do not think you would find was popular in the law courts of Christian countries. I have known in my time quite a number of judges who were very earnest Christians, and they none of them felt that they were acting contrary to Christian principles in what they did. Then Christ says: 'Give to him that asketh thee, and from him that would borrow of thee turn not thou away.' That is very good principle. . . .

Then there is one other maxim of Christ which I think has a great deal in it, but I do not find that it is very popular among some of our Christian friends. He says: 'If thou wilt be perfect, go and sell that thou hast, and give to the poor.' That is a very excellent

[2] Stanley Baldwin.

maxim, but, as I say, it is not much practised. All these, I think, are good maxims, although they are a little difficult to live up to. I do not profess to live up to them myself but then after all, it is not quite the same thing as for a Christian.

DEFECTS IN CHRIST'S TEACHING

Having granted the excellence of these maxims, I come to certain points in which I do not believe that one can grant either the super- lative wisdom or the superlative goodness of Christ as depicted in the Gospels; and here I may say that one is not concerned with the historical question. Historically it is quite doubtful whether Christ ever existed at all, and if He did we do not know anything about Him, so that I am not concerned with the historical question, which is a very difficult one. I am concerned with Christ as He appears in the Gospels, taking the Gospel narrative as it stands, and there one does find some things that do not seem to be very wise. For one thing, He certainly thought that His Second Coming would occur in clouds of glory before the death of all the people who were living at that time. There are a great many texts that prove that. He says, for instance: 'Ye shall not have gone over the cities of Israel, till the Son of Man be come.' Then He says: 'There are some standing here which shall not taste death till the Son of Man comes into His Kingdom'; and there are a lot of places where it is quite clear that He believed that His Second Coming would happen during the lifetime of many then living. That was the belief of His earlier followers, and it was the basis of a good deal of His moral teach- ing. When He said, 'Take no thought for the morrow', and things of that sort, it was very largely because He thought that the Second Coming was going to be very soon, and that all ordinary mundane affairs did not count. I have, as a matter of fact, known some Christians who did believe that the Second Coming was imminent. I knew a parson who frightened his congregation terribly by telling them that the Second Coming was very imminent indeed, but they were much consoled when they found that he was planting trees in his garden. The early Christians did really believe it, and they did abstain from such things as planting trees in their gardens, because they did accept from Christ the belief that the Second Coming was imminent. In that respect clearly He was not so wise as some other people have been, and He was certainly not superlatively wise.

THE MORAL PROBLEM

Then you come to moral questions. There is one very serious defect to my mind in Christ's moral character, and that is that He believed in hell. I do not myself feel that any person who is really profoundly humane can believe in everlasting punishment. Christ certainly as depicted in the Gospels did believe in everlasting punishment, and one does find repeatedly a vindictive fury against those people who would not listen to His preaching – an attitude which is not uncommon with preachers, but which does somewhat detract from superlative excellence. You do not, for instance, find that attitude in Socrates. You find him quite bland and urbane towards the people who would not listen to him; and it is, to my mind, far more worthy of a sage to take that line than to take the line of indignation. You probably all remember the sort of things that Socrates was saying when he was dying,[3] and the sort of things that he generally did say to people who did not agree with him.

You will find that in the Gospels Christ said: 'Ye serpents, ye generation of vipers, how can ye escape the damnation of hell?' That was said to people who did not like His preaching. It is not really to my mind quite the best tone, and there are a great many of these things about hell. There is, of course, the familiar text about the sin against the Holy Ghost: 'Whosoever speaketh against the Holy Ghost it shall not be forgiven him neither in this world nor in the world to come.' That text has caused an unspeakable amount of misery in the world, for all sorts of people have imagined that they have committed the sin against the Holy Ghost, and thought that it would not be forgiven them either in this world or in the world to come. I really do not think that a person with a proper degree of kindliness in his nature would have put fears and terrors of that sort into the world.

Then Christ says: 'The Son of Man shall send forth His angels, and they shall gather out of His kingdom all things that offend, and them which do iniquity, and shall cast them into a furnace of fire; there shall be wailing and gnashing of teeth'; and He goes on about the wailing and gnashing of teeth. It comes in one verse after another, and it is quite manifest to the reader that there is a certain pleasure in contemplating wailing and gnashing of teeth, or else it

[3] (See Plato, *The Last Days of Socrates*, translated and edited by H. Treddenick (Penguin 1954)—ed.)

would not occur so often. Then you all, of course, remember about the sheep and the goats; how at the Second Coming to divide the sheep and the goats He is going to say to the goats: 'Depart from me, ye cursed, into everlasting fire.' He continues: 'And these shall go away into everlasting fire.' Then He says again: 'If thy hand offend thee, cut it off; it is better for thee to enter into life maimed, than having two hands to go into hell, into the fire that never shall be quenched; where the worm dieth not and the fire is not quenched.' He repeats that again and again also. I must say that I think all this doctrine, that hell-fire is a punishment for sin, is a doctrine of cruelty. It is a doctrine that put cruelty into the world and gave the world generations of cruel torture; and the Christ of the Gospels, if you could take Him as His chroniclers represent Him, would certainly have to be considered partly responsible for that.

There are other things of less importance. There is the instance of the Gadarene swine where it certainly was not very kind to the pigs to put the devils into them and make them rush down the hill to the sea. You must remember that He was omnipotent, and He could have made the devils simply go away; but He chooses to send them into the pigs. Then there is the curious story of the fig-tree, which always rather puzzled me. You remember what happened about the fig-tree. 'He was hungry; and seeing a fig-tree afar off having leaves, He came if haply He might find anything thereon; and when He came to it He found nothing but leaves, for the time of figs was not yet. And Jesus answered and said unto it: "No man eat fruit of thee hereafter for ever", . . . and Peter . . . saith unto Him: "Master, behold the fig-tree which thou cursedst is withered away." ' This is a very curious story, because it was not the right time of year for figs, and you really could not blame the tree. I cannot myself feel that either in the matter of wisdom or in the matter of virtue Christ stands quite as high as some other people known to history. I think I should put Buddha and Socrates above Him in those respects.

THE EMOTIONAL FACTOR

As I said before, I do not think that the real reason why people accept religion has anything to do with argumentation. They accept religion on emotional grounds. One is often told that it is a very wrong thing to attack religion, because religion makes men virtuous. So I am told; I have not noticed it. . . .

That is the idea – that we should all be wicked if we did not hold to the Christian religion. It seems to me that the people who have held to it have been for the most part extremely wicked. You find this curious fact, that the more intense has been the religion of any period and the more profound has been the dogmatic belief, the greater has been the cruelty and the worse has been the state of affairs. In the so-called ages of faith, when men really did believe the Christian religion in all its completeness, there was the Inquisition, with its tortures; there were millions of unfortunate women burnt as witches; and there was every kind of cruelty practised upon all sorts of people in the name of religion.

You find as you look around the world that every single bit of progress in humane feeling, every improvement in the criminal law, every step towards the diminution of war, every step towards better treatment of the coloured races, or every mitigation of slavery, every moral progress that there has been in the world, has been consistently opposed by the organised Churches of the world. I say quite deliberately that the Christian religion, as organised in its Churches, has been and still is the principal enemy of moral progress in the world.

HOW THE CHURCHES HAVE RETARDED PROGRESS

You may think that I am going too far when I say that that is still so. I do not think that I am. Take one fact. You will bear with me if I mention it. It is not a pleasant fact, but the Churches compel one to mention facts that are not pleasant. Supposing that in this world that we live in today an inexperienced girl is married to a syphilitic man, in that case the Catholic Church says: 'This is an indissoluble sacrament. You must stay together for life.' And no steps of any sort must be taken by that women to prevent herself from giving birth to syphilitic children. That is what the Catholic Church says. I say that that is fiendish cruelty, and nobody whose natural sympathies have not been warped by dogma, or whose moral nature was not absolutely dead to all sense of suffering, could maintain that it is right and proper that that state of things should continue.

That is only one example. There are a great many ways in which at the present moment the Church, by its insistence upon what it chooses to call morality, inflicts upon all sorts of people undeserved and unnecessary suffering. And of course, as we know, it is in its major part an opponent still of progress and of improvement in all the ways that diminish suffering in the world, because it has chosen to label as morality a certain narrow set of rules of conduct which have nothing to do with human happiness; and when you say that this or that ought to be done because it would make for human happiness, they think that has nothing to do with the matter at all. 'What has human happiness to do with morals? The object of morals is not to make people happy.'

FEAR THE FOUNDATION OF RELIGION

Religion is based, I think, primarily and mainly upon fear. It is partly the terror of the unknown, and partly, as I have said, the wish to feel that you have a kind of elder brother who will stand by you in all your troubles and disputes. Fear is the basis of the whole thing – fear of the mysterious, fear of defeat, fear of death. Fear is the parent of cruelty, and therefore it is no wonder if cruelty and religion have gone hand-in-hand. It is because fear is at the basis of those two things. In this world we can now begin a little to understand things, and a little to master them by the help of science, which has forced its way step by step against the Christian religion, against the Churches, and against the opposition of all the old precepts. Science can help us to get over this craven fear in which mankind has lived for so many generations. Science can teach us, and I think our own hearts can teach us, no longer to look round for imaginary supports, no longer to invent allies in the sky, but rather to look to our own efforts here below to make this world a fit place to live in, instead of the sort of place that the Churches in all these centuries have made it.

WHAT WE MUST DO

We want to stand upon our own feet and look fair and square at the world – its good facts, its bad facts, its beauties, and its ugliness; see the world as it is, and be not afraid of it. Conquer the world by intelligence, and not merely by being slavishly subdued by the terror that comes from it. The whole conception of God is a conception derived from the ancient oriental despotisms. It is a conception quite unworthy of free men. When you hear people in church debasing themselves and saying that they are miserable sinners, and all the rest of it, it seems contemptible and not worthy of self-respecting human beings. We ought to stand up and look the world frankly in the face. We ought to make the best we can of the world, and if it is not so good as we wish, after all it will still be better than what these others have made of it in all these ages. A good world needs knowledge, kindliness, and courage; it does not need a regretful hankering after the past, or a fettering of the free intelligence by the words uttered long ago by ignorant men. It needs a fearless outlook and a free intelligence. It needs hope for the future, not looking back all the time towards a past that is dead, which we trust will be far surpassed by the future that our intelligence can create.

Chapter 6

Christian Ethics[1]

'Marriage,' says Westermarck, 'is rooted in family rather than family in marriage.'[2] This view would have been a truism in pre-Christian times, but since the advent of Christianity it has become an important proposition needing to be stated with emphasis. Christianity, and more particularly St Paul, introduced an entirely novel view of marriage, that it existed not primarily for the procreation of children, but to prevent the sin of fornication.

The views of St Paul on marriage are set forth, with a clarity that leaves nothing to be desired, in the First Epistle to the Corinthians. The Corinthian Christians, one gathers, had adopted the curious practice of having illicit relations with their stepmothers (I Cor. 5: 1), and he felt the situation needed to be dealt with emphatically. The views which he set forth are as follows:[3]

1. Now concerning the things whereof ye wrote unto me: It is good for a man not to touch a woman.
2. Nevertheless, to avoid fornication, let every man have his own wife, and let every woman have her own husband.
3. Let the husband render unto the wife due benevolence: and likewise also the wife unto the husband.
4. The wife hath not power of her own body, but the husband: and likewise also the husband hath not power of his own body, but the wife.
5. Defraud ye not one the other, except it be with consent for a time, that ye may give yourselves to fasting and prayer; and come together again, that Satan tempt you not for your incontinency.
6. But I speak this by permission, and not of commandment.
7. For I would that all men were even as I myself. But every

[1] From *Marriage and Morals* (1929), pp 26–35.
[2] E. Westermarck, *History of Human Marriage* (Macmillan 1891).
[3] I Cor. 7: 1–9.

man hath his proper gift of God, one after this manner, and another after that.

8. I say therefore to the unmarried and widows, It is good for them if they abide even as I.

9. But if they cannot contain, let them marry; for it is better to marry than to burn.

It will be seen that in this passage St Paul makes no mention whatever of children: the biological purpose of marriage appears to him wholly unimportant. This is quite natural, since he imagined that the Second Coming was imminent and that the world would soon come to an end. At the Second Coming men were to be divided into sheep and goats, and the only thing of real importance was to find oneself among the sheep on that occasion. St Paul holds that sexual intercourse, even in marriage, is something of a handicap in the attempt to win salvation (I Cor. 8: 32–4). Nevertheless it is possible for married people to be saved, but fornication is deadly sin, and the unrepentant fornicator is sure to find himself among the goats. I remember once being advised by a doctor to abandon the practice of smoking, and he said that I should find it easier if, whenever the desire came upon me, I proceeded to suck an acid drop. It is in this spirit that St Paul recommends marriage. He does not suggest that it is quite as pleasant as fornication, but he thinks it may enable the weaker brethren to withstand temptation; he does not suggest for a moment that there may be any positive good in marriage, or that affection between husband and wife may be a beautiful and desirable thing, nor does he take the slightest interest in the family; fornication holds the centre of the stage in his thoughts, and the whole of his sexual ethics is arranged with reference to it. It is just as if one were to maintain that the sole reason for baking bread is to prevent people from stealing cake. St Paul does not deign to tell us why he thinks fornication so wicked. One is inclined to suspect that, having thrown over the Mosaic Law, and being therefore at liberty to eat pork, he wishes to show that his morality is nevertheless quite as severe as that of orthodox Jews. Perhaps the long ages during which pork had been prohibited had made it seem to the Jews as delicious as fornication, and therefore he would need to be emphatic as regards the ascetic elements in his creed.

Condemnation of all fornication was a novelty in the Christian religion. The Old Testament, like most codes of early civilisation, forbids adultery, but it means by adultery intercourse with a married woman. This is evident to anyone who reads the Old Testament attentively. For example, when Abraham goes to Egypt with Sarah he tells the king that Sarah is his sister, and the king, believing this, takes her into his harem; when it subsequently transpires that she is Abraham's wife, the king is shocked to find that he has unwittingly committed sin, and reproaches Abraham for not having told him the facts. This was the usual code of antiquity. A woman who had intercourse outside marriage was thought ill of, but a man was not condemned unless he had intercourse with the wife of another, in which case he was guilty of an offence against property. The Christian view that all intercourse outside marriage is immoral was, as we see in the above passages from St Paul, based upon the view that all sexual intercourse, even within marriage, is regrettable. A view of this sort, which goes against biological facts, can only be regarded by sane people as a morbid aberration. The fact that it is embedded in Christian ethics has made Christianity, throughout its whole history, a force tending towards mental disorders and unwholesome views of life. . . .

It is clear that the whole system of Christian ethics, both in the Catholic and the Protestant forms, requires to be re-examined, as far as possible without the preconceptions to which a Christian education predisposes most of us. Emphatic and reiterated assertion, especially during childhood, produces in most people a belief so firm as to have a hold even over the unconscious, and many of us who imagine that our attitude towards orthodoxy is quite emancipated are still, in fact, subconsciously controlled by its teachings. We must ask ourselves quite frankly what led the Church to condemn all fornication. Do we think that it had valid grounds for this condemnation? Or, if we do not, are there grounds, other than those adduced by the Church, which ought to lead us to the same conclusion? The attitude of the early Church was that there is something essentially impure in the sexual act, although this act must be excused when it is performed after fulfilling certain preliminary conditions. This attitude in itself must be regarded as purely superstitious; the reasons which led to its adoption were presumably those which were considered in the last chapter as liable to cause an anti-sexual attitude, that is to say, those who first inculcated such a view must have suffered from a diseased condition of body or mind, or both. The fact that an opinion has been widely held

is no evidence whatever that it is not utterly absurd; indeed, in view
of the silliness of the majority of mankind, a widespread belief is
more likely to be foolish than sensible. The Pelew Islanders believe
that the perforation of the nose is necessary for winning eternal
bliss.[4] Europeans think that this end is better attained by wetting
the head while pronouncing certain words. The belief of the Pelew
Islanders is a superstition; the belief of the Europeans is one of the
truths of our holy religion. ...

The Christian ethics inevitably, through the emphasis laid upon
sexual virtue, did a great deal to degrade the position of women.
Since the moralists were men, woman appeared as the temptress;
if they had been women, man would have had this role. Since
woman was the temptress, it was desirable to curtail her opportunities for leading men into temptation; consequently respectable
women were more hedged about with restrictions, while the women
who were not respectable, being regarded as sinful, were treated
with the utmost contumely. It is only in quite modern times that
women have regained the degree of freedom which they enjoyed
in the Roman Empire. The patriarchal system . . . did much to
enslave women, but a great deal of this was undone just before
the rise of Christianity. After Constantine, women's freedom was
again curtailed under the pretence of protecting them from sin. It
is only with the decay of the notion of sin in modern times that
women have begun to regain their freedom.

The writings of the Fathers are full of invectives against Woman.

Woman was represented as the door of hell, as the mother of
all human ills. She should be ashamed at the very thought that
she is a woman. She should live in continual penance, on account
of the curses she has brought upon the world. She should be
ashamed of her dress, for it is the memorial of her fall. She
should be especially ashamed of her beauty, for it is the most
potent instrument of the daemon. Physical beauty was indeed
perpetually the theme of ecclesiastical denunciations, though
one singular exception seems to have been made; for it has
been observed that in the Middle Ages the personal beauty of
bishops was continually noticed upon their tombs. Women were
even forbidden by a provincial Council, in the sixth century, on
account of their impurity, to receive the Eucharist into their naked

---

[4] Westermarck, op. cit., p. 170.

hands. Their essentially subordinate position was continually maintained.[5]

The laws of property and inheritance were altered in the same sense against women, and it was only through the freethinkers of the French Revolution that daughters recovered their rights of inheritance.

[5] W. E. Lecky, *History of European Morals*, 6th revised edn, (Longman 1884), vol. ii, pp. 357–8.

Further Readings

RUSSELL

'Religion and the Churches' in *Principles of Social Reconstruction*
'Religion in Education' in *Education and the Social Order*
'On the Value of Scepticism' in *Sceptical Essays*
'Has Religion Made Useful Contributions to Civilisation?' in *Why I am Not a Christian*
'What I Believe', ibid.
'Can Religion Cure our Troubles?', ibid.
'The Existence of God—a debate between Bertrand Russell and Father F. C. Copleston, S. J.', ibid.
'Do We Survive Death?', ibid.

OTHER AUTHORS

Cupitt, Don, *Crisis of Moral Authority* (Lutterworth Press 1972)
Figes, Eva, 'A Man's God' in *Patriarchal Attitudes* (Faber & Faber 1970)
Hick, J. H., *Arguments for the Existence of God* (Macmillan 1970)
Vidler, A. R. (ed.), *Objections to Christian Belief* (Pelican 1965)

Part Three

War and
World Government

Introduction

It should be clear from the following selections that Russell's pacifism was not one of faith but, as Peter Mayer calls it, 'a pacifism of expedience'.[1] Russell was sometimes charged with inconsistency in his pacifist stance, for although he spoke out against the prosecution of the First World War and against nuclear warfare, he was not averse to the use of force against the Germany of Hitler and in 1948 even suggested that the United States should threaten to declare war on Russia for the purpose of forcing nuclear disarmament upon her.[2] But Russell's was not a pacifism of principle, such as that of the early Chinese philosophers Lao-tze and Confucius, who held that the use of force is never justified, or that of such Christian sects as the Quakers and the Jehovah Witnesses, who regard warfare as totally incompatible with Christian teachings. Russell writes:

> I have never been a complete pacifist and have at no time maintained that all who wage war are to be condemned. I have held the view, which I should have thought was that of common sense, that some wars have been justified and others not. . . . I do not deny that the policy that I have advocated has changed from time to time. It has changed as circumstances have changed. To achieve a single purpose, sane men adapt their policies to the circumstances.[3]

Russell regarded force, or the threat of it, as justified in circumstances where it provides the best means of protecting the human race against a return to barbarism or complete annihilation. He thought the First World War was likely to put civilisation back many hundreds of years, and for this reason advocated an early cessation of hostilities (see Chapter 7) – for this reason also he wrote to

---

[1] P. Mayer (ed.), *The Pacifist Conscience*. (For full references to this and other works mentioned, see the list of Further Readings on p. 112.)
[2] See *Autobiography of Bertrand Russell*, vol. III, p. 18.
[3] *Common Sense and Nuclear Warfare*, pp. 90–1.

President Wilson asking that America forcibly intervene to end the war.[4] His later appeal for the threat of war on Russia is explicable in this light as well: he felt that this was at the time a likely way of halting the arms race and eliminating the possibility of a world holocaust. When Russia, and later China, had built up their own nuclear forces, he proclaimed the end of all warfare as the only guarantee for the survival of the human race.

THE THREAT OF NATIONALISM

Russell writes: 'Devotion to the nation is perhaps the deepest and most widespread religion of the present age'; if the world is to be saved, 'men must first face the terrible realisation that the gods before whom they have bowed down were false gods' (Chapter 7). Here Russell identifies *nationalism*, a fairly new phenomenon in history dating from the eighteenth century and the French Revolution, as the greatest present threat to civilisation. War indeed, and the preparation for it, is one of the primary functions of the modern State, and patriotic zeal is encouraged in State education to the extent that most men are willing to die for their country and believe the myth of its superior excellence over all others. (See also 'War as an Institution' and 'Patriotism in Education'.) Because nationalism presents this threat, Russell and other pacifists have seen the creation of a single World State as the only solution; pacifism and internationalism have for the most part gone hand in hand.[5]

Various forms of World Government have been suggested, and some even tried; yet those that have been tried were ineffective in preventing wars. The League of Nations, dating from 1919, excluded Germany, Russia, Austria and Turkey – and the United States was not represented at the beginning. Furthermore, when Russia finally joined she was expelled again in 1939 for hostilities towards Finland. The United Nations Organisation, replacing the League of Nations in 1944, has always been fraught with difficulties: the exclusion of China for many years, the veto power of certain states in the Security Council, and the unwillingness of the major world powers to allow equal say to the numerous smaller emergent states, have been the greatest obstacles to its success. The International Court of Justice (the Hague Court), established in the Charter

[4] See *Autobiography of Bertrand Russell*, vol. III, p. 28.
[5] See the papers collected in Mayer, op. cit.

of the United Nations, has been just as unsuccessful in providing legal remedies to disputes between states, for disputes can only be adjudicated with the consent of the states involved, and even then there remains no way of enforcing the decisions of the Court. The United States is one power that accepts the jurisdiction of the Hague Court, but this has had little effect on the world situation, for in accordance with the infamous 'Connally Amendment' the right is reserved to withold from the Court disputes that she regards as falling within her own jurisdiction – such as Vietnam.

AN IDEAL WORLD GOVERNMENT

These previous approaches to a World Government had one fundamental drawback in common, namely that under each of them individual states retained their own 'deterrents'. The major feature of Russell's proposal is that World Government be the sole possessor of weapons of mass destruction, with the military capacity to enforce a solution to disputes involving even the largest of the present powers (Chapter 9). This feature understood, his proposal is for a Federation of existing nations, these nations being represented in the World Government in accordance with their populations; nations will also be grouped in subordinate federations with other nations having similar interests and political structures. The function of the World Government being to prevent war, 'separate nations should preserve their autonomy in everything that did not concern war or peace', and where nations are joined in subordinate federations, 'the World Authority should take cognisance only of the external relations of federations and not of the relations between different states in one federation unless a risk of war was involved or some unconstitutional action'. In furthering its aim of preventing war, the World Government will however be entitled to control education in the various states to the extent of inhibiting nationalist fervour, encouraging instead allegiance to 'the brotherhood of man'; it will also work to promote economic equality in different parts of the world.

COMMENTS

Russell's form of World Government should be compared with those advocated by other writers and the case in its favour made clear. For example, in *De Monarchia* (1310) Dante proposed a Universal Federation which would guarantee peace by having a single ruler: this would perhaps have the desired effect but would bring with it certain evils, for no power would remain vested in the conquered nations. (At times Russell actually saw this type of World Government, or something very similar to it, as a possible escape route from the evils of warfare – see, for example, his letter to President Wilson mentioned above.) An alternative suggestion is that of William O. Douglas in *Towards a Global Federalism*. Douglas champions a reformed United Nations in which all parties are willing to submit to the Rule of Law rather than the Rule of Force; though that body would lack the military might to enforce its decisions, Douglas apparently holds that the leading powers would accept them as the condition of their security in the nuclear age. Russell's proposals are obviously based upon a more pessimistic view of man's nature, and though the United Nations has performed many good services so far (not only in matters of international disputes but also through such agencies as UNESCO and the Food and Agricultural Organisation), crises like the Cuban missile affair and the Sino-Indian border dispute possibly argue for a more powerful World Government. A form even stronger than the one Russell favours is proposed by Mortimer Lipsky in *Never Again War* – a World Government that is not international in the sense of a federation of continuing nation states but a single world legislative body, a Parliament of Man:

> As a prerequisite for the formation of a true world government, nation states must be effaced from the globe and swept into the dustbin, the rubbish dump, of history. So that mankind might live, France must cease to be France, the United States cease to be the United States, the Soviet Union cease to be the Soviet Union. The blood-stained flags of the 135 nation states must be lowered from their standards and the white flag of a united world unfurled.[6]

Lipsky arrives at this solution from a premiss he holds in common with Russell: the nation, 'more sacred than civilisation, humanity, family, religion, friendship, decency', is the great curse of the age. Why then does Russell not arrive at the same conclusion?

[6] Lipsky, op. cit., p. 213.

What can be said in favour of separate nations preserving their autonomy in whatever does not concern war or peace, if the State presents the threat of war? Russell argues, correctly, that the State has certain positive functions, such as the substitution of law for force, the provision of education and general welfare requirements like sanitation, the encouragement of scientific research: but these functions could be met by a single World State. A second reason could be one of expediency: if the World Government is to be brought about by co-operation between present powers, it is unlikely that those powers would be willing to forfeit their sovereignty completely.[7] Other reasons might be given, but perhaps the most pressing for Russell concerns the theme of man's liberty, which (as we saw in Part One) he holds to be very closely related to devolution of authority, and for this reason the World State is to take upon itself only those duties that cannot be passed down to a lower body.

But could the remaining nations be relied upon to accept graciously the loss of military power? Russell believed that a fundamental change of outlook was necessary for the happiness of the human race, indeed for its very existence in the future: in *Principles of Social Reconstruction* he claimed that those impulses that make for life are to be encouraged over the possessive ones that are embodied in the State, war and property. Yet a World Government such as he outlines might be made to work if the nation state came to mean something different from a unit of power in international affairs, to embody instead the impulses to life. This shift of emphasis is well expressed in Senator Fulbright's 'idea mankind can hold to': 'that the nation performs its essential function not in its capacity as a *power*, but in its capacity as a *society*, or, to put it simply, that the primary business of the nation is not itself but its people.'[8]

QUESTIONS

1. Are there any circumstances in which war (or the threat of war) is justified?
2. 'When we say, "Britons never, never, never shall be slaves"

---

[7] As Lipsky realises: op. cit., p. 230.
[8] J. W. Fulbright, *The Arrogance of Power*, p. 245.

our hearts swell with pride and we feel, though we do not explicitly say, that we should be slaves if we were not free at any moment to commit any crime against any country.' Is this mere cynicism?

3. Under what conditions, if any, would you be prepared to advocate the form of World Government that Lipsky describes?

Chapter 7

The Case for Pacifism[1]

The war has grown, in the main, out of the life of impulse, not out
of reason or desire. There is an impulse of aggression, and an
impulse of resistance to aggression. Either may, on occasion, be
in accordance with reason, but both are operative in many cases in
which they are quite contrary to reason. Each impulse produces a
whole harvest of attendant beliefs. The beliefs appropriate to the
impulse of aggression may be seen in Bernhardi, or in the early
Mohammedan conquerors, or, in full perfection, in the Book of
Joshua. There is first of all a conviction of the superior excellence
of one's own group, a certainty that they are in some sense the
chosen people. This justifies the feeling that only the good and
evil of one's own group is of real importance, and that the rest
of the world is to be regarded merely as material for the triumph
or salvation of the higher race. In modern politics this attitude is
embodied in imperialism. Europe as a whole has this attitude
towards Asia and Africa, and many Germans have this attitude
towards the rest of Europe.

Correlative to the impulse of aggression is the impulse of
resistance to aggression. This impulse is exemplified in the attitude
of the Israelites to the Philistines or of medieval Europe to the
Mohammedans. The beliefs which it produces are beliefs in the
peculiar wickedness of those whose aggression is feared, and in
the immense value of national customs which they might suppress
if they were victorious. When the war broke out, all the reactionaries
in England and France began to speak of the danger to democracy,
although until that moment they had opposed democracy with all
their strength. They were not insincere in so speaking: the impulse
of resistance to Germany made them value whatever was endangered
by the German attack. They loved democracy because they hated

[1] From *Principles of Social Reconstruction* (1916), pp. 15–19, 68–71,
76–7.

Germany; but they thought they hated Germany because they loved democracy.

The correlative impulses of aggression and resistance to aggression have both been operative in all the countries engaged in the war. Those who have not been dominated by one or other of these impulses may be roughly divided into three classes. There are, first, men whose national sentiment is antagonistic to the State to which they are subject. This class includes some Irish, Poles, Finns, Jews, and other members of oppressed nations. From our point of view, these men may be omitted from our consideration, since they have the same impulsive nature as those who fight, and differ merely in external circumstances.

The second class of men who have not been part of the force supporting the war have been those whose impulsive nature is more or less atrophied. Opponents of pacifism suppose that all pacifists belong to this class, except when they are in German pay. It is thought that pacifists are bloodless, men without passions, men who can look on and reason with cold detachment while their brothers are giving their lives for their country. Among those who are merely passively pacifist, and do no more than abstain from actively taking part in the war, there may be a certain proportion of whom this is true. I think the supporters of war would be right in decrying such men. In spite of all the destruction which is wrought by the impulses that lead to war, there is more hope for a nation which has these impulses than for a nation in which all impulse is dead. Impulse is the expression of life, and while it exists there is hope of its turning towards life instead of death; but lack of impulse is death, and out of death no new life will come.

The active pacifists, however, are not of this class: they are not men without impulsive force, but men in whom some impulse to which war is hostile is strong enough to overcome the impulses that lead to war. It is not the act of a passionless man to throw himself athwart the whole movement of the national life, to urge an outwardly hopeless cause, to incur obloquy and to resist the contagion of collective emotion. The impulse to avoid the hostility of public opinion is one of the strongest in human nature, and can only be overcome by an unusual force of direct and uncalculating impulse; it is not cold reason alone that can prompt such an act.

Impulses may be divided into those that make for life and those that make for death. The impulses embodied in the war are among those that make for death. Any one of the impulses that make for life, if it is strong enough, will lead a man to stand out against the war. Some of these impulses are only strong in highly civilised men; some are part of common humanity. The impulses towards art and science are among the more civilised of those that make for life. Many artists have remained wholly untouched by the passions of the war, not from feebleness of feeling, but because the creative instinct, the pursuit of a vision, makes them critical of the assaults of national passion, and not responsive to the myth in which the impulse of pugnacity clothes itself. And the few men in whom the scientific impulse is dominant have noticed the rival myths of warring groups, and have been led through understanding to neutrality. But it is not out of such refined impulses that a popular force can be generated which shall be sufficient to transform the world.

There are three forces on the side of life which require no exceptional mental endowment, which are not very rare at present, and might be very common under better social institutions. They are love, the instinct of constructiveness, and the joy of life. All three are checked and enfeebled at present by the conditions under which men live – not only the less outwardly fortunate, but also the majority of the well-to-do. Our institutions rest upon injustice and authority: it is only by closing our hearts against sympathy and our minds against truth that we can endure the oppressions and unfairnesses by which we profit. The conventional conception of what constitutes success leads most men to live a life in which their most vital impulses are sacrificed, and the joy of life is lost in listless weariness. Our economic system compels almost all men to carry out the purposes of others rather than their own, making them feel impotent in action and only able to secure a certain modicum of passive pleasure. All these things destroy the vigour of the community, the expansive affections of individuals, and the power of viewing the world generously. All these things are unnecessary and can be ended by wisdom and courage. If they were ended, the impulsive life of men would become wholly different, and the human race might travel towards a new happiness and a new vigour. . . .

The problem for the reflective pacifist is twofold: how to keep

G

his own country at peace, and how to preserve the peace of the world. It is impossible that the peace of the world should be preserved while nations are liable to the mood in which Germany entered upon the war – unless, indeed, one nation were so obviously stronger than all others combined as to make war unnecessary for that one and hopeless for all the others. As this war has dragged on its weary length, many people must have asked themselves whether national independence is worth the price that has to be paid for it. Would it not perhaps be better to secure universal peace by the supremacy of one Power? 'To secure peace by a world federation' – so a submissive pacifist might have argued during the first two years of the war – 'would require some faint glimmerings of reason in rulers and peoples, and is therefore out of the question; but to secure it by allowing Germany to dictate terms to Europe would be easy. Since there is no other way of ending war' – so our advocate of peace at any price would contend – 'let us adopt this way, which happens at the moment to be open to us.' It is worth while to consider this view more attentively than it is commonly considered.

There is one great historic example of a long peace secured in this way; I mean the Roman Empire. We in England boast of the *Pax Britannica* which we have imposed, in this way, upon the warring races and religions in India. If we are right in boasting of this, if we have in fact conferred a benefit upon India by enforced peace, the Germans would be right in boasting if they could impose a *pax Germanica* upon Europe. Before the war, men might have said that India and Europe are not analogous, because India is less civilised than Europe; but now, I hope, no one would have the effrontery to maintain anything so preposterous. Repeatedly in modern history there has been a chance of achieving European unity by the hegemony of a single State; but always England, in obedience to the doctrine of the Balance of Power, has prevented this consummation, and preserved what our statesmen have called the 'liberties of Europe'. It is this task upon which we are now engaged. But I do not think our statesmen, or any others among us, have made much effort to consider whether the task is worth what it costs.

In one case we were clearly wrong: in our resistance to revolutionary France. If revolutionary France could have conquered the Continent and Great Britain, the world would now be happier, more civilised, and more free, as well as more peaceful. But revolutionary France was a quite exceptional case, because its early conquests were made in the name of liberty, against tyrants, not against peoples; and everywhere the French armies were welcomed as liberators by all except rulers and bigots. In the case of Philip II we were as clearly right as we were wrong in 1793. But in both cases our action is not to be judged by some abstract diplomatic conception of the 'liberties of Europe', but by the ideals of the Power seeking hegemony, and by the probable effect upon the welfare of ordinary men and women throughout Europe.

'Hegemony' is a very vague word, and everything turns upon the degree of interference with liberty which it involves. There is a degree of interference with liberty which is fatal to many forms of national life; for example, Italy in the seventeenth and eighteenth centuries was crushed by the supremacy of Spain and Austria. If the Germans were actually to annex French provinces, as they did in 1871, they would probably inflict a serious injury upon those provinces, and make them less fruitful for civilisation in general. For such reasons national liberty is a matter of real importance, and a Europe actually governed by Germany would probably be very dead and unproductive. But if 'hegemony' merely means increased weight in diplomatic questions, more coaling stations and possessions in Africa, more power of securing advantageous commercial treaties, then it can hardly be supposed that it would do any vital damage to other nations; certainly it would not do so much damage as the present war is doing. I cannot doubt that, before the war, a hegemony of this kind would have abundantly satisfied the Germans. But the effect of the war, so far, has been to increase immeasurably all the dangers which it was intended to avert. We have now only the choice between certain exhaustion of Europe in fighting Germany and possible damage to the national life of France by German tyranny. Stated in terms of civilisation and human welfare, not in terms of national prestige, that is now in fact the issue.

Assuming that war is not ended by one State conquering all the others, the only way in which it can be permanently ended is by a world federation. So long as there are many sovereign States, each with its own Army, there can be no security that there will not be war. There will have to be in the world only one Army and one Navy before there will be any reason to think that wars have ceased. This means that, so far as the military functions of the

State are concerned, there will be only one State, which will be worldwide. . . .

War is surrounded with glamour, by tradition, by Homer and the Old Testament, by early education, by elaborate myths as to the importance of the issues involved, by the heorism and self-sacrifice which these myths call out. Jephthah sacrificing his daughter is a heroic figure, but he would have let her live if he had not been deceived by a myth. Mothers sending their sons to the battlefield are heroic, but they are as much deceived as Jephthah. And, in both cases alike, the heroism which issues in cruelty would be dispelled if there were not some strain of barbarism in the imaginative outlook from which myths spring. A God who can be pleased by the sacrifice of an innocent girl could only be worshipped by men to whom the thought of receiving such a sacrifice is not wholly abhorrent. A nation which believes that its welfare can only be secured by suffering and inflicting hundreds of thousands of equally horrible sacrifices, is a nation which has no very spiritual conception of what constitutes national welfare. It would be better a hundredfold to forgo material comfort, power, pomp, and outward glory than to kill and be killed, to hate and be hated, to throw away in a mad moment of fury the bright heritage of the ages. We have learnt gradually to free our God from the savagery with which the primitive Israelites and the Fathers endowed Him: few of us now believe that it is His pleasure to torture most of the human race in an eternity of hell-fire. But we have not yet learnt to free our national ideals from the ancient taint. Devotion to the nation is perhaps the deepest and most widespread religion of the present age. Like the ancient religions, it demands its persecutions, its holocausts, its lurid heroic cruelties; like them, it is noble, primitive, brutal, and mad. Now, as in the past, religion, lagging behind private consciences through the weight of tradition, steels the hearts of men against mercy and their minds against truth. If the world is to be saved, men must learn to be noble without being cruel, to be filled with faith and yet open to truth, to be inspired by great purposes without hating those who try to thwart them. But before this can happen, men must first face the terrible realisation that the gods before whom they have bowed down were false gods and the sacrifices they have made were vain.

Chapter 8

The Future of Mankind[1]

Before the end of the present century, unless something quite unforeseeable occurs, one of three possibilities will have been realised. These three are:

1. The end of human life, perhaps of all life on our planet.
2. A reversion to barbarism after a catastrophic diminution of the population of the globe.
3. A unification of the world under a single government, possessing a monopoly of all the major weapons of war.

I do not pretend to know which of these will happen, or even which is the most likely. What I do contend, without any hesitation, is that the kind of system to which we have been accustomed cannot possibly continue.

The first possibility, the extinction of the human race, is not to be expected in the next world war, unless that war is postponed for a longer time than now seems probable. But if the next world war is indecisive, or if the victors are unwise, and if organised states survive it, a period of feverish technical development may be expected to follow its conclusion. With vastly more powerful means of utilising atomic energy than those now available, it is thought by many sober men of science that radio-active clouds, drifting round the world, may disintegrate living tissue everywhere. Although the last survivor may proclaim himself universal Emperor, his reign will be brief and his subjects will all be corpses. With his death the uneasy episode of life will end, and the peaceful rocks will revolve unchanged until the sun explodes.

Perhaps a disinterested spectator would consider this the most desirable consummation, in view of man's long record of folly and cruelty. But we, who are actors in the drama, who are entangled in the net of private affections and public hopes, can hardly take this attitude with any sincerity. True, I have heard men say that

[1] From *Unpopular Essays* (1950), pp. 38–42.

they would prefer the end of man to submission to the Soviet Government, and doubtless in Russia there are those who would say the same about submission to Western capitalism. But this is rhetoric with a bogus air of heroism. Although it must be regarded as unimaginative humbug, it is dangerous, because it makes men less energetic in seeking ways of avoiding the catastrophe that they pretend not to dread.

The second possibility, that of a reversion to barbarism, would leave open the likelihood of a gradual return to civilisation, as after the fall of Rome. The sudden transition will, if it occurs, be infinitely painful to those who experience it, and for some centuries afterwards life will be hard and drab. But at any rate there will still be a future for mankind, and the possibility of rational hope.

I think such an outcome of a really scientific world war is by no means improbable. Imagine each side in a position to destroy the chief cities and centres of industry of the enemy; imagine an almost complete obliteration of laboratories and libraries, accompanied by a heavy casualty rate among men of science; imagine famine due to radio-active spray, and pestilence caused by bacteriological warfare: would social cohesion survive such strains? Would not prophets tell the maddened populations that their ills were wholly due to science, and that the extermination of all educated men would bring the millennium? Extreme hopes are born of extreme misery, and in such a world hopes could only be irrational. I think the great states to which we are accustomed would break up, and the sparse survivors would revert to a primitive village economy.

The third possibility, that of the establishment of a single government for the whole world, might be realised in various ways: by the victory of the United States in the next world war, or by the victory of the USSR, or, theoretically, by agreement. Or – and I think this is the most hopeful of the issues that are in any degree probable – by an alliance of the nations that desire an international government, becoming, in the end, so strong that Russia would no longer dare to stand out. This might conceivably be achieved without another world war, but it would require courageous and imaginative statesmanship in a number of countries.

There are various arguments that are used against the project of a single government of the whole world. The commonest is that the project is utopian and impossible. Those who use this argument, like most of those who advocate a World Government, are thinking of a World Government brought about by agreement. I think it is plain that the mutual suspicions between Russia and the West make it futile to hope, in any near future, for any genuine agreement. Any pretended universal authority to which both sides can agree, as things stand, is bound to be a sham, like UNO. Consider the difficulties that have been encountered in the much more modest project of an international control over atomic energy, to which Russia will only consent if inspection is subject to the veto, and therefore a farce. I think we should admit that a World Government will have to be imposed by force.

But – many people will say – why all this talk about a World Government? Wars have occurred ever since men were organised into units larger than the family, but the human race has survived. Why should it not continue to survive even if wars go on occurring from time to time? Moreover, people like war, and will feel frustrated without it. And without war there will be no adequate opportunity for heroism or self-sacrifice.

This point of view – which is that of innumerable elderly gentlemen, including the rulers of Soviet Russia – fails to take account of modern technical possibilities. I think civilisation could probably survive one more world war, provided it occurs fairly soon and does not last long. But if there is no slowing up in the rate of discovery and invention and if great wars continue to recur, the destruction to be expected, even if it fails to exterminate the human race, is pretty certain to produce the kind of reversion to a primitive social system that I spoke of a moment ago. And this will entail such an enormous diminution of population, not only by war, but by subsequent starvation and disease, that the survivors are bound to be fierce and, at least for a considerable time, destitute of the qualities required for rebuilding civilisation.

Nor is it reasonable to hope that, if nothing drastic is done, wars will nevertheless not occur. They always have occurred from time to time, and obviously will break out again sooner or later unless mankind adopt some system that makes them impossible. But the only such system is a single government with a monopoly of armed force.

If things are allowed to drift, it is obvious that the bickering between Russia and the Western democracies will continue until Russia has a considerable store of atomic bombs, and that when that time comes there will be an atomic war. In such a war, even if the worst consequences are avoided, Western Europe, including Great Britain, will be virtually exterminated. If America and the USSR survive as organised states, they will presently fight again. If one side is victorious, it will rule the world, and a unitary government of mankind will have come into existence; if not, either mankind, or at least civilisation, will perish. This is what must happen if nations and their rulers are lacking in constructive vision.

When I speak of 'constructive vision', I do not mean merely the theoretical realisation that a World Government is desirable. More than half the American nation, according to the Gallup poll, hold this opinion. But most of its advocates think of it as something to be established by friendly negotiation, and shrink from any suggestion of the use of force. In this I think they are mistaken. I am sure that force, or the threat of force, will be necessary. I hope the threat of force may suffice, but, if not, actual force should be employed.

Assuming a monopoly of armed force established by the victory of one side in a war between the US and the USSR, what sort of world will result?

In either case, it will be a world in which successful rebellion will be impossible. Although, of course, sporadic assassination will still be liable to occur, the concentration of all important weapons in the hands of the victors will make them irresistible, and there will therefore be secure peace. Even if the dominant nation is completely devoid of altruism, its leading inhabitants, at least, will achieve a very high level of material comfort, and will be freed from the tyranny of fear. They are likely, therefore, to become gradually more good-natured and less inclined to persecute. Like the Romans, they will, in the course of time, extend citizenship to the vanquished. There will then be a true world state, and it will be possible to forget that it will have owed its origin to conquest. Which of us, during the reign of Lloyd George, felt humiliated by the contrast with the days of Edward I?

A world empire of either the US or the USSR is therefore preferable to the results of a continuation of the present international anarchy.

Chapter 9

An Outline of World Government[1]

A World Government of a sort might be created without securing world peace. This might happen, for example, if the various nations which contributed to the armed force of the World Authority did so by supplying national contingents which might retain their national unity and, at a crisis, might be loyal to their national Government rather than to the World Authority. It may be worth while to give an outline of a possible World Constitution especially designed to obviate such dangers. Such an outline is, of course, only a suggestion, and emphatically not a prophecy. My purpose is merely to show that a World Constitution which would prevent war is possible.

A World Authority, if it is to fulfil its function, must have a legislature and an executive and irresistible military power. Irresistible military power is the most essential condition and also the most difficult to fulfil. I will, therefore, deal with it first.

All nations would have to agree to reduce national armed forces to the level necessary for internal police action. No nation should be allowed to retain nuclear weapons or any other means of whole-sale destruction. The World Authority should have power to recruit in every country and to manufacture such weapons as might be deemed essential. In a world where separate nations were disarmed, the military forces of the World Authority would not need to be very large and would not constitute an onerous burden upon the various constituent nations. In order to prevent the development of national loyalties in any part of the international forces, it would be necessary that each fairly large unit should be of mixed nationality. There should not be European contingents or Asian contingents or African contingents or American contingents, but there should be everywhere, as far as possible, a balanced mixture. The higher commands should, as far as possible, be given to men from small countries which could not entertain any

---

[1] From *Has Man a Future?* (1961), pp. 78–82.

hope of world dominion. There would, of course, have to be a right of inspection by the World Government to make sure that the disarmament provisions in every country were obeyed.

The constitution of the legislature would, of course, be federal. Separate nations should preserve their autonomy in everything that did not concern war or peace. There is, in any federal constitution, a difficulty where the units are of very different sizes. Should each unit have the same voice, or should voting power be proportional to population? In America, as everyone knows, an ingenious compromise was adopted: one principle governed the Senate and the other the House of Representatives. I think, however, that a different principle would work better in constructing the world legislature. I think there should be subordinate federations of approximately equal population. These should be constructed, as far as possible, so as to be fairly homogeneous and to have many common interests. Wherever a number of States were combined in one of these subordinate federations, the World Authority should take cognisance only of the external relations of federations and not of the relations between different States in one federation unless a risk of war was involved or some unconstitutional action.

How these federations should be constituted would no doubt vary with the time that the constitution was enacted. If it were enacted at the present time, one might suggest some such arrangement as the following: (1) China; (2) India and Ceylon; (3) Japan and Indonesia; (4) The Mohammedan world from Pakistan to Morocco; (5) Equatorial Africa; (6) the USSR and Satellites; (7) Western Europe, Britain, Ireland, and Australia and New Zealand; (8) the United States and Canada; (9) Latin America. Some countries which do not come in this division present difficulties. For example, Yugoslavia, Israel, South Africa, and Korea. It is impossible to guess, in advance, what might, at any given moment, be the best arrangement for such countries. Each federation should be represented in the world legislature in proportion to its population. There would have to be both a world constitution setting out the relations of the subordinate federations to the world federation, and also a constitution of each subordinate federation guaranteed by the world federation. The World Government would support subordinate federations and their constituent States in any constitutional action. It should only interfere with the internal affairs of the subordinate federations in the event of a federation engaging in some unconstitutional action; and the same principle should apply to the relations between a subordinate federation and its constituent national States.

What should be the powers of the world legislature? In the first place, no treaty should be valid unless confirmed by the legislature, which should also have power to revise existing treaties if new circumstances made this advisable. The legislature should also have the right to object to violently nationalist systems of education such as might be considered to constitute a danger to peace.

There would need to be, also, an executive which, I think, should be responsible to the legislature. Its main function, apart from maintaining the armed forces, should be to declare any violation of the world constitution by any national State or combination of States and, if necessary, to inflict punishment for such violation.

There is one other matter of very considerable importance, and that is international law. At present, international law has very little force. It would be essential that a legal institution like the Hague Court should have the same authority as belongs to national courts. I think, further, that there should be an international criminal law for dealing with men who have committed crimes that were popular in their own country. In the Nuremberg Trials, it was impossible to feel the justice of sentences inflicted as a result of victory in war, although it was also clear that there ought to have been a legal method of punishing at least some of those who were condemned.

I think that, if such an International Authority is to be successful in diminishing motives towards warlike feelings, it will have to work to promote a continual approach towards economic equality in the standard of life of different parts of the world. So long as there as rich countries and poor countries, there will be envy on the one side and possible economic oppression on the other. A continual attempt to move towards economic equality must, therefore, be part of the pursuit of secure and lasting peace.

Chapter 10

Why World Government is Disliked[1]

It is objections to the kind of system suggested in the preceding chapter that I am now concerned to consider. Much the strongest objections arise from the sentiment of nationalism. When we say, 'Britons never, never never shall be slaves', our hearts swell with pride and we feel, though we do not explicitly say, that we should be slaves if we were not free at any moment to commit any crime against any other country. The feeling in favour of national freedom is one which has been rapidly increasing throughout the last 150 years, and, if World Government is to be inaugurated, it will have to take account of this sentiment and do whatever is possible to satisfy it.

The men who argue in favour of unrestricted national freedom do not realise that the same reasons would justify unrestricted individual freedom. I will not yield to Patrick Henry, or anyone else, in love of freedom, but, if there is to be as much freedom in the world as possible, it is necessary that there should be restrictions preventing violent assaults upon the freedom of others. In the internal affairs of States this is recognised: murder is everywhere made illegal. If the law against murder were repealed, the liberty of all except murderers would be diminished, and even the liberty of murderers would, in most cases, be short-lived, since they would soon be murdered. But, although everyone, except a few anarchists, admits this as regards the relations of an individual to his national State, there is immense reluctance to admit it as regards the relations of national States to the world at large.

It is true that attempts have been made, ever since the time of Grotius, to create a body of international law. These attempts have been wholly admirable; and, in so far as international law has commanded general respect, it has been useful. But it has remained optional with each national State to respect or not respect codes of international law. Law is a farce unless there is power to

[1] From *Has Man a Future?* (1961), pp. 83–9.

enforce it, and power to enforce international law against great States is impossible while each possesses vast armaments. Great States have, at present, the privilege of killing members of other States whenever they feel so disposed, though this liberty is disguised as the heroic privilege of dying in defence of what is right and just. Patriots always talk of dying for their country, and never of killing for their country.

War has so long been a part of human life that it is difficult for our feelings and our imaginations to grasp that the present anarchic national freedoms are likely to result in freedom only for corpses. If institutions could be created which would prevent war, there would be much more freedom in the world than there is at present, just as there is more freedom owing to the prevention of individual murder.

Nevertheless, while the sentiment of nationalism remains as strong as it is at present, effective restrictions of the national sovereignty will continue to be distasteful to a great many people. Suppose, for example, that there was only one navy in the world, and that its supreme admiral should be chosen in rotation from the various participating Powers. Most patriotic Britons would exclaim: 'What, should the British Navy, which Nelson led to glory, come in due course to be commanded by a Russian! Perish the thought!' And after this exclamation, the man who had made it would become impervious to further argument. He would go on to point out that an international force might be employed against his own country. Most countries have, at one time or another, committed acts which a World Government would have to pronounce criminal, and some of the worst offenders in this respect have been admired by people who considered themselves liberal. The most noteworthy example in history is the admiration of Napoleon by men like Byron and Heine. Before a World Government becomes possible, it will be necessary that men be made to realise the impossibility of international anarchy while modern weapons of mass destruction exist. This is a difficult task and is not rendered easier by the opposition of powerful Governments.

Another objection to World Government which is at present very powerful, especially in Communist countries, is that it might stereotype the *status quo*. So long as the opposition between Communists and anti-Communists remains as fierce as it is at present, it will be difficult to win assent to any international institutions which might seem likely to impede the transition of individual nations from one camp to the other. It would, of course, be possible to decree that each nation should be free to arrange its own economy in whatever way it pleased, but it might prove exceedingly difficult to secure that this liberty should be genuinely respected. If World Government is to be successfully established, there will have to be much more tolerance than there is at present between different kinds of national government. It will be necessary to forgo some part of the pleasures of national self-assertion. Each nation may continue to *think*, as each nation does at present, that it is superior to all other nations in every essential respect, but, when nations meet for purposes of negotiation, the negotiators will have to restrain the public expression of their feelings of superiority within the limits of courtesy. Such restraint would not be easy while national sentiments remain as strong as they are at present.

There is another argument which is often used against World Government. It is said, and widely believed, that it would bring a new danger of military tyranny. What would prevent the international armed force from making a military insurrection, and installing its generalissimo as Emperor of the World? Those who bring up this argument fail to realise that exactly the same problem exists at present in every national State. It is a very real problem, and in many countries, though not in the most civilised, military tyrannies have been established by unconstitutional methods. But in the leading countries of the world, control over the military by the civil authorities has been pretty successfully maintained. When Lincoln was appointing a Commander-in-Chief, over the Northern forces in the American Civil War, he was warned that the candidate whom he favoured would seek dictatorship. Lincoln wrote to him, mentioning these fears, and added: 'The way to become a dictator is to win victories. I shall look to you for the victories, and I will risk the dictatorship.' Events proved that this was a wise decision. In the conflict in England over the Reform Bill, Wellington was passionately opposed to reform, but, in spite of his immense reputation, it never occurred to him to lead the Army against Parliament. In Russia, when Stalin turned against a number of generals, he had no difficulty in having them executed. The superiority of the civil government over the armed forces in the USSR has been complete ever since the end of the civil war which gave power to the Soviet Government. There is no reason to suppose that it would be more difficult to keep the military in order under a World Government than it is under national governments. The danger is one of which the civil government would have to be aware, but there is no reason to think that the methods which would be developed for combating the danger would be less successful than they have proved in the great States of the present day.

There would have to be, everywhere, but especially in the armed forces, a vigorous inculcation of loyalty to the World Government. If, as was suggested in the previous chapter, every large unit in the armed forces was of completely mixed nationality, it would be difficult, if not impossible, for a faction to generate a spirit of nationalistic revolt.

There is one rather grave psychological obstacle to the establishment of a World Government. It is that there would be no outside enemy to fear. Social cohesion, in so far as it is instinctive, is mainly promoted by a common danger or a common enmity. This is most obvious where a grown-up person is in charge of a number of unruly children. So long as everything remains quiet, it is difficult to get the children to obey, but if anything frightening happens, such as a bad thunderstorm or a fierce dog, the children instantly seek the protection of the grown-up and become completely obedient. The same sort of thing applies to adults, though not quite so obviously. Patriotism is far more intense in time of war than at other times, and there is a readiness to obey even onerous governmental decrees which is absent when there is secure peace. A World Government, since it would have no external human enemies, would not be able to invoke quite this motive for loyalty. I think it would be necessary, as an essential part of education, to remind people of the dangers that would still remain, such as poverty and malnutrition and epidemics, and, also, to make them aware that, if loyalty to the World Government failed, scientific war might once more become probable. Although hatred of foreign nations promotes social cohesion more easily, perhaps, than anything else, it would be unduly pessimistic to suppose that nothing more positive and more beneficial could take its place. This whole matter is one which depends more upon education than upon anything else.

Further Readings

RUSSELL

'The State', chap. 2 of *Principles of Social Reconstruction*
'War as an Institution', chap. 3 of *Principles of Social Reconstruction*
'Patriotism in Education' in *Education and the Social Order*
Common Sense and Nuclear Warfare
Has Man a Future?
Autobiography of Bertrand Russell, vol. III, 1944–67

OTHER AUTHORS

Douglas, W. O., *Towards a Global Federalism* (University of London Press 1968)
Fulbright, J. W., *The Arrogance of Power* (Jonathan Cape 1967, Pelican 1970)
Lipsky, M., *Never Again War: The Case for World Government* (Thomas Yoseloff 1971)
Mayer, P. (ed.), *The Pacifist Conscience* (Rupert Hart-Davis 1966)
Pauling, Linus, *No More War* (Gollancz 1958)
Schweitzer, Albert, *Peace or Atomic War* (Adam and Charles Black 1958)

Part Four

Philosophy

Introduction

I have so far said little about Russell's work as a philosopher in the academic sense, and it is perhaps primarily for this work that he will be remembered as one of this century's most brilliant men. His greatest contributions to philosophy – especially those concerning the nature of mathematics – require a considerable background of study to be fully understood; however the general outlines of his aims and achievements can easily be made clear.

RUSSELL'S PROBLEM: THE SEARCH FOR CERTAINTY

Russell sets out the kind of problems that occupied him in his academic work in the introduction to *My Philosophical Development*:

> My original interest in philosophy had two sources. On the one hand, I was anxious to discover whether philosophy would provide any defence for anything that could be called religious belief, however vague; on the other hand, I wished to persuade myself that something could be known, in pure mathematics if not elswhere. I thought about both these problems during adolescence, in solitude and with little help from books. As regards religion, I came to disbelieve first in free will, then in immortality, and finally in God. As regards the foundations of mathematics, I got nowhere.[1]

Russell's concern in philosophy remained the same throughout his long career: what, if anything, can be known with certainty? His reflections on religion bore fruit in such popular works as *Why I am Not a Christian*, while his desire to find some body of propositions which we can know with certainty led him to the study of mathematics – for surely if anything can be certainly known the truths of mathematics can.

Russell published *The Principles of Mathematics* in 1903, and

[1] *My Philosophical Development* (1959), p. 11.

the first of the three volumes of his monumental *Principia Mathematica* in 1910, followed by the more popularly styled *Introduction to Mathematical Philosophy* in 1919 (which he wrote while confined in Brixton prison for his pacifist activities). *Principia Mathematica* had as co-author A. N. Whitehead, one of Russell's mathematics teachers at Cambridge, and Russell was always the last to underrate his contribution to it though it is clear that the greatest themes are due to Russell himself: 'The problems with which we had to contend were of two sorts: philosophical and mathematical. Broadly speaking, Whitehead left the philosophical problems to me. As for the mathematical problems, Whitehead invented most of the notation, except in so far as it was taken over from Peano.'[2]

The aim of *Principia Mathematica* was 'to show that all pure mathematics follows from purely logical premisses and uses only concepts definable in logical terms'. Here Russell was working on the same problem as the great German mathematician Gottlob Frege, though at the beginning unaware of Frege's existence: to show that mathematics has the same nature as logic, indeed that it is one branch of that subject, and hence has the *certainty* that we can attribute to such logical propositions as 'Either it is raining or it is not raining'.

Russell's ambitious scheme required a number of steps:[3] firstly, the development of a wholly new form of logic; next, the definition of mathematical notions in terms of this new logic; and finally the derivation of mathematical propositions such as 'Two plus two equals four' from the non-mathematical logical ones like 'Either (some proposition) p is true or p is not true'. Though this third step, that of derivation, took most of the seven years needed to complete the project, the first two steps demanded the inventiveness and insight that makes the book a classic of modern thought.

REDUCING MATHEMATICS TO LOGIC

Although attempts had been made by men such as Leibniz, Boole and Peirce to develop a new and more adequate kind of logic, Aristotelian logic was still the accepted form at the time. Russell's logic differed from this by countenancing more forms of proposition or

[2] *My Philosophical Development*, p. 74.
[3] See *My Philosophical Development*, chapters 6–8, for a general account.

statement than the simple subject-predicate form: whereas Aristotelian logic treated, for example, the proposition 'All Greeks are mortal' as on a par with such a subject-predicate proposition as 'Socrates is mortal', Russell recognised its form as being more complex – in fact, its true logical form is best exhibited by writing it as 'If anything is a Greek then it is mortal'. In the new 'mathematical logic' that Russell developed, a number of different logical forms are distinguished, and certain relations between propositions that were not expressible in Aristotelian logic could now be expressed. But further than this, Russell and Whitehead proceeded to 'axiomatise' the propositions of logic, by giving a few simple logical propositions as axioms and showing how the rest could be derived from them. (Compare the way in which geometry is presented as an axiomatised system in Euclid's formulation.) Russell's achievements even in this part of *Principia Mathematica* alone have earned him the lasting admiration of logicians coming after him.

The second and crucial stage of Russell's project was that of the definition of mathematical notions (the cardinal numbers, ordinal numbers, etc.) in terms of logical ones (such as those expressed by the words 'and', 'or', 'not', and 'all'). The Italian logician G. Peano, whom Russell had met in 1900 at a conference in Paris, had already succeeded in reducing arithmetic to an axiomatised form; in his system the axioms expressed relationships between the basic notions on which arithmetic depends, and the rest of classical arithmetic could be derived from these. It rested with Russell to show that these axioms could be *derived* from the propositions of his logical system when an interpretation of the arithmetical notions in terms of logical ones was given. His procedure was to effect definitions of these notions by means of the logical notion of a class, or set: Peano himself had in fact used this latter notion in his own axiom system, but had kept it distinct from what he saw as the peculiarly mathematical ones; it was Russell's aim to show that the latter are indeed not peculiarly mathematical at all, but logical. When this was achieved, arithmetic would have been reduced to logic, and arithmetical propositions would have been shown to be certain.

Whether or not Russell actually succeeded in the grand task of *Principia Mathematica*, his attempt has undoubtedly lasting philosophical importance. The new logic, his treatment of the notion of a class and definition of numbers in terms of it, and the celebrated Theory of Types and Theory of Descriptions were some of the outcomes of this struggle. This last, the Theory of Descriptions, has been called a 'paradigm of philosophy'; and Russell's work was a great stimulus to the famous 'Viennese Circle' of philosophers, the Logical Positivists.

OCCAM'S RAZOR

Turning now to the other landmarks in Russell's philosophical career, we see the continuation of his desire to find a body of certain knowledge in his study of sense-perception and the nature of the self. One principle that he laid great stress on was 'Occam's razor' (the principle that 'entities are not to be multiplied without necessity'), which he expressed as: 'wherever possible, logical constructions are to be substituted for inferred entities'. In the context of a search for certainty the importance of Occam's razor is easily seen: if you can take a body of beliefs and reconstruct it in such a manner that fewer things are assumed to exist than before, you have removed one possibility of error in those beliefs and put them on firmer ground. For example, if you could say all that we now say about atoms, molecules, and so forth, but *interpret* what you say in such a manner that you do not have to assume that these microscopic entities actually *exist* (in which case you are treating them as 'logical fictions'), you are less open to error through not assuming so much about the world. Occam's razor became of considerable importance to Russell in his search for certain knowledge, for in accordance with it he came to regard his task as that of reconstructing our knowledge, in particular that knowledge of the external world gained through the senses. In extolling the virtues of his definitions of arithmetical terms in *Principia*, he wrote:

> But much more important than either of these two advantages is the fact that we get rid of numbers as metaphysical entities. They become, in fact, merely linguistic conveniences with no more substantiality than belongs to 'etc.' or 'i.e.'. Kronecker, in philosophising about mathematics, said that God made the integers and the mathematicians made the rest of the mathematical apparatus'. . . . With the above definition of numbers

this prerogative of the integers disappears and the primitive apparatus of the mathematician is reduced to such purely logical terms as *or, not, all* and *some*. This was my first experience of the usefulness of Occam's razor in diminishing the number of undefined terms and unproved propositions required in a given body of knowledge.[4]

In 1912 appeared *The Problems of Philosophy*,[5] a little book still regarded as one of the best introductions to the subject and one in which Russell made plain his concern for certain knowledge. It was followed in 1914 by the publication of his Lowell Lectures, *Our Knowledge of the External World*: the purpose of these lectures was to effect the reconstruction of knowledge obtained through perception without making the assumption of a world existing independently of the perceiver. In 1921 came his *Analysis of Mind*, the message of which was that 'matter is not so material and mind not so mental as is generally supposed', for here he attempted to show that the self, or mind, can be exhibited also as a logical fiction, indeed can be constructed out of sensations. It was in this book that Russell came closest to the 'neutral monism' theory of William James, a theory that supposed no ultimate difference between mind and matter.

The programme of reconstruction was not without problems, however, and in the Tarner Lectures delivered at Trinity in 1925 he had to go back on the results of the Lowell Lectures, returning to a theory of perception that allowed independent existence to the physical world. These lectures were published in 1927 as *An Analysis of Matter*. He treated the problems of perception again in *Human Knowledge: Its Scope and Limits*, the outcome of lectures delivered at Cambridge and published in 1948. This book also contains his fullest account of the justification of the basic principles of science, and its fame rests mainly on this.

One further philosophical work that should receive a mention is *An Inquiry into Meaning and Truth*, published in 1940, and concerned with the meaning of words and the various accounts people have given of the nature of truth. Russell's most famous work, and financially the most successful, is the vast *History of Western Philosophy*, which came out in 1946, just two years after

[4] *My Philosophical Development*, p. 71.
[5] See below, Chapters 11, 12 and 13.

the volume of the 'Library of Living Philosophers' devoted to various studies of his works by other philosophers. His last philosophical book was *My Philosophical Development*, published in 1959.

I want now to concentrate on an examination of the extracts reproduced here. These extracts are not taken from Russell's writings on mathematics but from his discussions of the nature of our factual knowledge of the world. Chapters 11 and 12 are concerned with the knowledge we obtain about the world of physical objects by means of our senses, and Chapter 13 primarily with our knowledge of the future, though the principles in question there are relevant to any belief we have that is based upon incomplete evidence.

RUSSELL'S THESIS

In 'Appearance and Reality' (Chapter 11) Russell is concerned with establishing the following thesis: *What we directly perceive (see, touch, etc.) when we are sensibly aware of a physical object like a table, is not the table itself but a sense-datum.* To understand this we have to ask what he means by 'directly perceive' and by 'sense-datum'. We find, in fact, that these two notions are closely connected: by 'sense-datum' he means whatever we directly perceive, or 'the things that are immediately known in sensation', and he claims that they are such things as colours, sounds, smells, hardnesses, roughnesses, and so on. But what does he mean by 'directly perceive'? He gives no explicit definition, but the following explanation accords well with his use of the expression: if we perceive a thing, as opposed to perceiving something that thing has brought about, we are perceiving it directly. This much understood, we can now grasp what is expressed by his thesis. In the case of looking at the table, he is saying that what we directly see are such sense-data as colours and shapes, and that these things are neither the table itself nor really properties of the table. Just as it might be said that seeing a man on television is only directly seeing an image *of* the man, Russell is saying that seeing a table is only directly seeing sense-data which are perhaps somehow related to the table. And now we can ask for the arguments that are thought to support this strange conclusion.

Russell's arguments all turn on the relativity of sense-perception, that is on the fact that what we perceive is partially dependent on the state of the perceiver and the physical conditions under which perception takes place. Briefly they are as follows. (1) The colour a table appears to have depends on the way that light falls upon it, and so on the perspective from which it is viewed: hence, there is no *one* colour that it appears to have. (2) Its colour depends on the character of the light and on the spectator himself ('it will seem different by artificial light, or to a colour-blind man, or to a man wearing blue spectacles'); hence, the colour it appears to have is not an inherent property of the table. From these two short arguments Russell draws the further conclusion that the table indeed has no one particular colour: he points out that what we mean by *the* colour of the table is the colour it appears to have to a *normal* spectator under *normal* conditions, but 'to avoid favouritism, we are compelled to deny that, in itself, the table has any particular colour'. He goes on to give comparable arguments for the texture, shape and degree of hardness of the table. In the case of shape, he argues (3) that a 'rectangular' table has different shapes from different perspectives; therefore, the real shape of the table is something only inferred from what is actually seen. From these arguments he draws his conclusion: 'The real table, if there is one, is not the same as what we immediately experience by sight or touch or hearing.'

Many philosophers, both before and after Russell, have found such arguments convincing, but on a close examination they seem to contain a number of false moves. For example, in (1) Russell infers, from the fact that light is reflected differently from the surface as we change our position, that the table has no one apparent colour; we can admit the premiss, but does it really follow that a glossy brown surface does not appear brown? Again, he claims that there is something arbitrary about singling out any one colour as *the* colour of the table, but a little thought will show that, given that certain conditions *are* normal for us, (for example, that white light is the usual illumination), there is good reason for favouring the colour it has under those conditions. However, leaving these doubts aside, let us ask whether the relativity of sense-perception requires us to accept Russell's conclusion.

AN ALTERNATIVE

We can oppose to Russell's thesis a less extreme one, which is supported by the sort of considerations involved in (1) to (3) above: *we do not always see the table as it is.* The table has a certain colour and shape, and in normal conditions these will be apparent. However, conditions are sometimes not normal, and when the light is bad, or of an unusual colour, or when our eyes are not functioning properly (if we are colour-blind, tired, or have jaundice, for example), we fail to see the table as it is. We admit in all this that what properties the table appears to have are dependent upon factors other than the table itself, but we deny that it follows that they are not (in normal conditions) inherent in the table: and in particular, we deny that there are these other things called 'sense data' that interpose themselves between the table and us. Even in abnormal conditions, we see the *table,* only we do not see it as it is.

To arrive at Russell's more extreme conclusion, there are two assumptions that have to be made: (*a*) what we directly perceive cannot have properties that it does not appear to have, and (*b*) in all cases of perception what we perceive is always something of the same nature.[6] The importance of (*a*) is that it allows Russell to argue that, in abnormal circumstances, what is directly perceived is a sense-datum which really has those properties revealed by our senses; and (*b*) allows him to add that even in normal circumstances what we directly perceive are always sense-data. Only given these assumptions does Russell's thesis follow; that is to say, there is as much reason for accepting his thesis as there is for these assumptions. Moreover, there is really very little to be said on their behalf.

Being convinced of the existence of sense-data, Russell moves on to raise one of the great traditional problems of philosophy, that of the existence of an external world (see Chapter 12, 'The Existence of Matter').[7] 'Granted that we are certain of our own sense-data, have we,' he asks, 'any reason for regarding them as signs of the existence of something else, which we can call the

[6] Cf. A. J. Ayer, *The Problem of Knowledge*, p. 88. A good discussion of the sense-datum thesis is contained in J. L. Austin, *Sense and Sensibilia.* (See Further Readings on p. 142).

[7] For other discussions of this problem see the works by Wittgenstein, Moore, and Ayer cited in Further Readings.

physical object?' The conclusion he comes to is that *we can accept the existence of physical objects which are causally responsible for our sense-data, as a reasonable hypothesis*. We cannot prove it demonstratively ('there is no logical impossibility in the supposition that the whole of life is a dream'), but there are considerations leading us to adopt it. One such, Russell says, is that this hypothesis gives us a far simpler picture of the world than one in which sense-data alone are taken to exist (see the example about the cat in Chapter 12) – this is his main argument in favour of the hypothesis. Unfortunately, as it stands it is most inadequate, for it is just not true that 'every principle of simplicity urges us to adopt the natural view'. Occam's razor, bidding us accept the fewest possible kinds of existents, indeed urges us in the opposite direction, to deny the hypothesis and so arrive at a simpler view of the world in this sense. Simplicity, of course, is not so simple a notion that there is only one answer to the question which of two theories is the simpler.

A second reason, moreover, for taking Occam's razor into account is the one Russell himself was so eager to stress in his programme of reconstructing our knowledge on a firmer basis. A theory of perception that denied the existence of physical objects independent of sense-data, and understood statements concerning such objects as really about actual and possible sense-data, would at least appear to remove the gulf between ourselves and the external world. Such a theory is known as 'phenomenalism', whereas Russell's account in Chapter 12 is a 'causal theory' of perception. In fact, very soon after writing *The Problems of Philosophy* Russell came to develop this alternative theory of phenomenalism.

WILL THE FUTURE BE LIKE THE PAST?

'On Induction' (Chapter 13) represents Russell's early treatment of another traditional problem of philosophy, the problem of the justification of inferences that are not logically conclusive (non-demonstrative, or inductive, inferences). Here he sets out a principle which he calls 'the principle of induction' (or 'the principle of the uniformity of nature') and makes the following two major claims: (1) it is a principle that is required to justify all those inferences that are not logically conclusive, whether they are made in ordinary life or in science; and (2) it must itself be accepted without a justification, for given that it is not logically true any attempt to justify it would involve inductive inference and hence be circular. The principle states essentially that *the more often things of a type A have been found to be associated with things of type B, given that they have never been found dissociated, the more certain we can be of finding the same association again.* Russell's position here accords with that adopted by David Hume in *A Treatise of Human Nature* (1739), who was the first philosopher to state this philosophical problem clearly, but few philosophers would now be willing to accept his claims without reservation. The main problems with Russell's first claim are, firstly, that it can be shown that his principle would justify inferences that we would not want to accept,[8] and secondly, that the principle is so general that it is hard to see just how it could support many of the inferences that we do accept. His second claim has also been criticised: Strawson (in *Introduction to Logical Theory*, p. 257), for example, denies that we can even ask for a justification of inductive inference: 'To ask whether it is reasonable to place reliance on inductive procedures is like asking whether it is reasonable to proportion the degree of one's convictions to the strength of the evidence. Doing this is what "being reasonable" *means* in such a context.' Again, philosophers like Nelson Goodman (in *Fact, Fiction and Forecast*) claim that the philosopher's task is not to seek a justification of induction but rather to describe the principles in accordance with which such inferences are made. Russell himself, in his later *Human Knowledge*, arrives at very much the same view, and there he sets out what he regards as the basic principles of inductive inference in a discussion far more subtle than this earlier treatment.[9]

QUESTIONS

1. 'To avoid favouritism, we are compelled to deny that, in itself, the table has any particular colour.' Explain as clearly as you can the importance of this remark in Russell's argument. What reasons can you think of for saying that we *should* call 'red' those things that appear red in normal circumstances?

[8] See A. J. Ayer, *Russell*, p. 94.
[9] See also *My Philosophical Development*, chap. 16.

2. When Macbeth thought he saw a dagger, surely there *was* something he saw (he did not see *nothing*). We could call what Macbeth saw a sense-datum; and surely the only difference between this case and those cases where we really do see daggers is that in those cases there are real daggers behind the sense-data. Discuss.

3. Russell's argument for the existence of physical objects lying behind sense-data is an argument from simplicity; an alternative hypothesis is that God is responsible for all the sense-data that appear to us. Why would Russell want to reject this alternative?

4. Will the sun rise tomorrow? How can we be sure?

Chapter 11

Appearance and Reality[1]

Is there any knowledge in the world which is so certain that no reasonable man could doubt it? This question, which at first sight might not seem difficult, is really one of the most difficult that can be asked. When we have realised the obstacles in the way of a straightforward and confident answer, we shall be well launched on the study of philosophy – for philosophy is merely the attempt to answer such ultimate questions, not carelessly and dogmatically, as we do in ordinary life and even in the sciences, but critically, after exploring all that makes such questions puzzling, and after realising all the vagueness and confusion that underlie our ordinary ideas.

In daily life, we assume as certain many things which, on a closer scrutiny, are found to be so full of apparent contradictions that only a great amount of thought enables us to know what it is that we really may believe. In the search for certainty, it is natural to begin with our present experiences, and in some sense, no doubt, knowledge is to be derived from them. But any statement as to what it is that our immediate experiences make us know is very likely to be wrong. It seems to me that I am now sitting in a chair, at a table of a certain shape, on which I see sheets of paper with writing or print. By turning my head I see out of the window buildings and clouds and the sun. I believe that the sun is about 93 million miles from the earth; that it is a hot globe many times bigger than the earth; that, owing to the earth's rotation, it rises every morning, and will continue to do so for an indefinite time in the future. I believe that, if any other normal person comes into my room, he will see the same chairs and tables and books and papers as I see, and that the table which I see is the same as the table which I feel pressing against my arm. All this seems to be so evident as to be hardly worth stating,

[1] From *The Problems of Philosophy* (1912), pp. 1–4 (Oxford University Press 1959).

except in answer to a man who doubts whether I know anything. Yet all this may be reasonably doubted, and all of it requires much careful discussion before we can be sure that we have stated it in a form that is wholly true.

To make our difficulties plain, let us concentrate attention on the table. To the eye it is oblong, brown, and shiny, to the touch it is smooth and cool and hard; when I tap it, it gives out a wooden sound. Anyone else who sees and feels and hears the table will agree with this description, so that it might seem as if no difficulty would arise; but as soon as we try to be more precise our troubles begin. Although I believe that the table is 'really' of the same colour all over, the parts that reflect the light look much brighter than the other parts, and some parts look white because of reflected light. I know that, if I move, the parts that reflect the light will be different, so that the apparent distribution of colours on the table will change. It follows that if several people are looking at the table at the same moment, no two of them will see exactly the same distribution of colours, because no two can see it from exactly the same point of view, and any change in the point of view makes some change in the way the light is reflected.

For most practical purposes these differences are unimportant, but to the painter they are all-important: the painter has to unlearn the habit of thinking that things seems to have the colour which common sense says they 'really' have, and to learn the habit of seeing things as they appear. Here we have already the beginning of one of the distinctions that cause most trouble in philosophy – the distinction between 'appearance' and 'reality', between what things seem to be and what they are. The painter wants to know what things seem to be, the practical man and the philosopher want to know what they are; but the philosopher's wish to know this is stronger than the practical man's, and is more troubled by knowledge as to the difficulties of answering the question.

To return to the table. It is evident from what we have found, that there is no colour which pre-eminently appears to be *the* colour of the table, or even of any particular part of the table – it appears to be of different colours from different points of view, and there is no reason for regarding some of these as more really its colour than others. And we know that even from a given point of view the colour will seem different by artificial light, or to a colour-blind man, or to a man wearing blue spectacles, while in the dark there will be no colour at all, though to touch and hearing the table will be unchanged. This colour is not something which is inherent in the table, but something depending upon the table and the spectator and the way the light falls on the table. When, in ordinary life, we speak of *the* colour of the table, we only mean the sort of colour which it will seem to have to a normal spectator from an ordinary point of view under usual conditions of light. But the other colours which appear under other conditions have just as good a right to be considered real; and therefore, to avoid favouritism, we are compelled to deny that, in itself, the table has any one particular colour.

The same thing applies to the texture. With the naked eye one can see the grain, but otherwise the table looks smooth and even. If we looked at it through a microscope, we should see roughnesses and hills and valleys, and all sorts of differences that are imperceptible to the naked eye. Which of these is the 'real' table? We are naturally tempted to say that what we see through the microscope is more real, but that in turn would be changed by a still more powerful microscope. If, then, we cannot trust what we see with the naked eye, why should we trust what we see through a microscope? Thus, again, the confidence in our senses with which we began deserts us.

The *shape* of the table is no better. We are all in the habit of judging as to the 'real' shape of things, and we do this so unreflectingly that we come to think we actually see the real shapes. But, in fact, as we all have to learn if we try to draw, a given thing looks different in shape from every different point of view. If our table is 'really' rectangular, it will look, from almost all points of view, as if it had two acute angles and two obtuse angles. If opposite sides are parallel, they will look as if they converged to a point away from the spectator; if they are of equal length, they will look as if the nearer side were longer. All these things are not commonly noticed in looking at a table, because experience has taught us to construct the 'real' shape from the apparent shape, and the 'real' shape is what interests us as practical men. But the 'real' shape is not what we see; it is something inferred from what we see. And what we see is constantly changing in shape as we move about the room; so that here again the senses seem not to give us the truth about the table itself, but only about the appearance of the table.

Similar difficulties arise when we consider the sense of touch. It is true that the table always gives us a sensation of hardness, and we feel that it resists pressure. But the sensation we obtain depends upon how hard we press the table and also upon what part of the body we press with; thus the various sensations due to various pressures or various parts of the body cannot be supposed to reveal *directly* any definite property of the table, but at most to be *signs* of some property which perhaps *causes* all the sensations, but is not actually apparent in any of them. And the same applies still more obviously to the sounds which can be elicited by rapping the table.

Thus it becomes evident that the real table, if there is one, is not the same as what we immediately experience by sight or touch or hearing. The real table, if there is one, is not *immediately* known to us at all, but must be an inference from what is immediately known. Hence, two very difficult questions, at once arise; namely, (1) Is there a table at all? (2) If so, what sort of object can it be?

It will help us in considering these questions to have a few simple terms of which the meaning is definite and clear. Let us give the name of 'sense-data' to the things that are immediately known in sensation: such things as colours, sounds, smells, hardnesses, roughnesses, and so on. We shall give the name 'sensation' to the experience of being immediately aware of these things. Thus, whenever we see a colour, we have a sensation *of* the colour, but the colour itself is a sense-datum, not a sensation. The colour is that *of* which we are immediately aware, and the awareness itself is the sensation. It is plain that if we are to know anything about the table, it must be by means of the sense-data – brown colour, oblong shape, smoothness, etc. – which we associate with the table; but, for the reasons which have been given, we cannot say that the table *is* the sense-data, or even that the sense-data are directly properties of the table. Thus a problem arises as to the relation of the sense-data to the real table, supposing there is such a thing.

The real table, if it exists, we will call a 'physical object'. Thus we have to consider the relation of sense-data to physical objects. The collection of all physical objects is called 'matter'. Thus our two questions may be restated as follows: (1) Is there any such thing as matter? (2) If so, what is its nature?

I

Chapter 12

The Existence of Matter[1]

In this chapter we have to ask ourselves whether, in any sense at all, there is such a thing as matter. Is there a table which has a certain intrinsic nature, and continues to exist when I am not looking, or is the table merely a product of my imagination, a dream-table, in a very prolonged dream? This question is of the greatest importance. For if we cannot be sure of the independent existence of objects, we cannot be sure of the independent existence of other people's bodies, and therefore still less of other people's minds, since we have no grounds for believing in their minds except such as are derived from observing their bodies. Thus if we cannot be sure of the independent existence of objects, we shall be left alone in a desert – it may be that the whole outer world is nothing but a dream, and that we alone exist. This is an uncomfortable possibility; but although it cannot be strictly *proved* to be false, there is not the slightest reason to suppose that it is true. In this chapter we have to see why this is the case.

Before we embark upon doubtful matters, let us try to find some more or less fixed point from which to start. Although we are doubting the physical existence of the table, we are not doubting the existence of the sense-data which made us think that there was a table; we are not doubting that, while we look, a certain colour and shape appear to us, and while we press, a certain sensation of hardness is experienced by us. All this, which is psychological, we are not calling in question. In fact, whatever else may be doubtful, some at least of our immediate experiences seem absolutely certain.

Descartes (1596–1650), the founder of modern philosophy, invented a method which may still be used with profit – the method of systematic doubt. He determined that he would believe nothing which he did not see quite clearly and distinctly to be true. What-

[1] From *The Problems of Philosophy* (1912), pp. 7–11 (Oxford University Press 1959).

ever he could bring himself to doubt, he would doubt, until he saw reason for not doubting it. By applying this method he gradually became convinced that the only existence of which he could be *quite* certain was his own. He imagined a deceitful demon, who presented unreal things to his senses in a perpetual phantasmagoria; it might be very improbable that such a demon existed, but still it was possible, and therefore doubt concerning things perceived by the senses was possible.

But doubt concerning his own existence was not possible, for if he did not exist, no demon could deceive him. If he doubted, he must exist; if he had any experiences whatever, he must exist. Thus his own existence was an absolute certainty to him. 'I think, therefore I am,' he said (*Cogito, ergo sum*); and on the basis of this certainty he set to work to build up again the world of knowledge which his doubt had laid in ruins. By inventing the method of doubt, and by showing that subjective things are the most certain, Descartes performed a great service to philosophy, and one which makes him still useful to all students of the subject. . . .

The problem we have to consider is this: granted that we are certain of our own sense-data, have we any reason for regarding them as signs of the existence of something else, which we can call the physical object? When we have enumerated all the sense-data which we should naturally regard as connected with the table, have we said all there is to say about the table, or is there still something else – something not a sense-datum, something which persists when we go out of the room? Common sense unhesitatingly answers that there is. What can be bought and sold and pushed about and have a cloth laid on it, and so on, cannot be a *mere* collection of sense-data. If the cloth completely hides the table, we shall derive no sense-data from the table, and therefore, if the table were merely sense-data, it would have ceased to exist, and the cloth would be suspended in empty air, resting, by a miracle, in the place where the table formerly was. This seems plainly absurd; but whoever wishes to become a philosopher must learn not to be frightened by absurdities.

One great reason why it is felt that we must secure a physical object in addition to the sense-data, is that we want the *same* object for different people. When ten people are sitting round a dinner-table, it seems preposterous to maintain that they are not seeing the same table-cloth, the same knives and forks and spoons and glasses. But the sense-data are private to each separate person; what is immediately present to the sight of one is not immediately present to the sight of another: they all see things from slightly different points of view, and therefore see them slightly differently. Thus, if there are to be public neutral objects, which can be in some sense known to many different people, there must be something over and above the private and particular sense-data which appear to various people. What reasons, then, have we for believing that there are such public neutral objects?

The first answer that naturally occurs to one is that, although different people may see the table slightly differently, still they all see more or less similar things when they look at the table, and the variations in what they see follow the laws of perspective and reflection of light, so that it is easy to arrive at a permanent object underlying all the different people's sense-data. I bought my table from the former occupant of my room; I could not buy *his* sense-data, which died when he went away, but I could and did buy the confident expectation of more or less similar sense-data. Thus it is the fact that different people have similar sense-data, and that one person in a given place at different times has similar sense-data, which makes us suppose that over and above the sense-data there is a permanent public object which underlies or causes the sense-data of various people at various times.

Now in so far as the above considerations depend upon supposing that there are other people besides ourselves, they beg the very question at issue. Other people are represented to me by certain sense-data, such as the sight of them or the sound of their voices, and if I had no reason to believe that there were physical objects independent of my sense-data, I should have no reason to believe that other people exist except as part of my dream. Thus, when we are trying to show that there must be objects independent of our own sense-data, we cannot appeal to the testimony of other people, since this testimony itself consists of sense-data, and does not reveal other people's experiences unless our own sense-data are signs of things existing independently of us. We must therefore, if possible, find, in our own purely private experiences, characteristics which show, or tend to show, that there are in the world things other than ourselves and our private experiences.

In one sense it must be admitted that we can never *prove* the existence of things other than ourselves and our experiences. No logical absurdity results from the hypothesis that the world consists of myself and my thoughts and feelings and sensations, and that everything else is mere fancy. In dreams a very complicated world may seem to be present, and yet on waking we find it was a delusion; that is to say, we find that the sense-data in the dream do not appear to have corresponded with such physical objects as we should naturally infer from our sense-data. (It is true that, when a physical world is assumed, it is possible to find physical causes for the sense-data in dreams: a door banging, for instance, may cause us to dream of a naval engagement. But although, in this case, there is a physical *cause* for the sense-data, there is not a physical object *corresponding* to the sense-data in the way in which an actual naval battle would correspond.) There is no logical impossibility in the supposition that the whole of life is a dream, in which we ourselves create all the objects that come before us. But although this is not logically impossible, there is no reason whatever to suppose that it is true; and it is, in fact, a less simple hypothesis, viewed as a means of accounting for the facts of our own life, than the common-sense hypothesis that there really are objects independent of us, whose action on us causes our sensations.

The way in which simplicity comes in from supposing that there really are physical objects is easily seen. If the cat appears at one moment in one part of the room, and at another in another part, it is natural to suppose that it has moved from the one to the other, passing over a series of intermediate positions. But if it is merely a set of sense-data, it cannot have ever been in any place where I did not see it; thus we shall have to suppose that it did not exist at all while I was not looking, but suddenly sprang into being in a new place. If the cat exists whether I see it or not, we can understand from our own experience how it gets hungry between one meal and the next; but if it does not exist when I am not seeing it, it seems odd that appetite should grow during non-existence as fast as during existence. And if the cat consists only of sense-data, it cannot be *hungry*, since no hunger but my own can be a sense-datum to me. Thus the behaviour of the sense-data which represent the cat to me, though it seems quite natural when regarded as an expression of hunger, becomes utterly inexplicable when regarded as mere movements and changes of patches of colour, which are as incapable of hunger as a triangle is of playing football.

But the difficulty in the case of the cat is nothing compared to the difficulty in the case of human beings. When human beings speak – that is, when we hear certain noises which we associate with ideas, and simultaneously see certain motions of lips and expressions of face – it is very difficult to suppose that what we hear is not the expression of a thought, as we know it would be if we emitted the same sounds. Of course similar things happen in dreams, where we are mistaken as to the existence of other people. But dreams are more or less suggested by what we call waking life, and are capable of being more or less accounted for on scientific principles if we assume that there really is a physical world. Thus every principle of simplicity urges us to adopt the natural view, that there really are objects other than ourselves and our sense-data which have an existence not dependent upon our perceiving them.

Chapter 13

On Induction[1]

In almost all our previous discussions we have been concerned
in the attempt to get clear as to our data in the way of knowledge of existence. What things are there in the universe whose
existence is known to us owing to our being acquainted with
them? So far, our answer has been that we are acquainted with
our sense-data, and, probably, with ourselves. These we know to
exist. And past sense-data which are remembered are known to
have existed in the past. This knowledge supplies our data.

But if we are to be able to draw inferences from these data –
if we are to know of the existence of matter, of other people, of
the past before our individual memory begins, or of the future,
we must know general principles of some kind by means of which
such inferences can be drawn. It must be known to us that the
existence of some one sort of thing, A, is a sign of the existence
of some other sort of thing, B, either at the same time as A or
at some earlier or later time, as, for example, thunder is a sign
of the earlier existence of lightning. If this were not known to
us, we could never extend our knowledge beyond the sphere of
our private experience; and this sphere, as we have seen, is exceedingly limited. The question we have now to consider is whether
such an extension is possible, and if so, how it is effected.

Let us take as an illustration a matter about which none of
us, in fact, feel the slightest doubt. We are all convinced that
the sun will rise tomorrow. Why? Is this belief a mere blind outcome of past experience, or can it be justified as a reasonable
belief? It is not easy to find a test by which to judge whether a
belief of this kind is reasonable or not, but we can at least ascertain
what sort of general beliefs would suffice, if true, to justify the
judgement that the sun will rise tomorrow, and the many other
similar judgements upon which our actions are based.

[1] From *The Problems of Philosophy* (1912), pp. 33–8 (Oxford University
Press 1959).

It is obvious that if we are asked why we believe that the sun will rise tomorrow, we shall naturally answer, 'Because it always has risen every day.' We have a firm belief that it will rise in the future, because it has risen in the past. If we are challenged as to why we believe that it will continue to rise as heretofore, we may appeal to the laws of motion: the earth, we shall say, is a freely rotating body, and such bodies do not cease to rotate unless something interferes from outside, and there is nothing outside to interfere with the earth between now and tomorrow. Of course it might be doubted whether we are quite certain that there is nothing outside to interfere, but this is not the interesting doubt. The interesting doubt is as to whether the laws of motion will remain in operation until tomorrow. If this doubt is raised, we find ourselves in the same position as when the doubt about the sunrise was first raised.

The *only* reason for believing that the laws of motion will remain in operation is that they have operated hitherto, so far as our knowledge of the past enables us to judge. It is true that we have a greater body of evidence from the past in favour of the laws of motion than we have in favour of the sunrise, because the sunrise is merely a particular case of fulfilment of the laws of motion, and there are countless other particular cases. But the real question is: do *any* number of cases of a law being fulfilled in the past afford evidence that it will be fulfilled in the future? If not, it becomes plain that we have no ground whatever for expecting the sun to rise tomorrow, or for expecting the bread we shall eat at our next meal not to poison us, or for any of the other scarcely conscious expectations that control our daily lives. It is to be observed that all such expectations are only *probable*; thus we have not to seek for a proof that they *must* be fulfilled, but only for some reason in favour of the view that they are *likely* to be fulfilled.

Now in dealing with this question we must, to begin with, make an important distinction, without which we should soon become involved in hopeless confusion. Experience has shown us that, hitherto, the frequent repetition of some uniform succession or coexistence has been a *cause* of our expecting the same succession or coexistence on the next occasion. Food that has a certain appearance generally has a certain taste, and it is a severe shock to our expectations when the familiar appearance is found to be associated with an unusual taste. Things which we see become associated, by habit, with certain tactile sensations which we expect if we touch them; one of the horrors of a ghost (in many ghost-stories) is that it fails to give us any sensations of touch. Uneducated people who go abroad for the first time are so surprised as to be incredulous when they find their native language not understood.

And this kind of association is not confined to men; in animals also it is very strong. A horse which has been driven often along a certain road resists the attempt to drive him in a different direction. Domestic animals expect food when they see the person who usually feeds them. We know that all these rather crude expectations of uniformity are liable to be misleading. The man who has fed the chicken every day throughout its life at last wrings its neck instead, showing that more refined views as to uniformity of nature would have been useful to the chicken.

But in spite of the misleadingness of such expectations, they nevertheless exist. The mere fact that something has happened a certain number of times causes animals and men to expect that it will happen again. Thus our instincts certainly cause us to believe that the sun will rise tomorrow, but we may be in no better a position than the chicken which unexpectedly has its neck wrung. We have therefore to distinguish the fact that past uniformities *cause* expectations as to the future, from the question whether there is any reasonable ground for giving weight to such expectations after the question of their validity has been raised.

The problem we have to discuss is whether there is any reason for believing in what is called 'the uniformity of nature'. The belief in the uniformity of nature is the belief that everything that has happened or will happen is an instance of some general law to which there are *no* exceptions. The crude expectations which we have been considering are all subject to exceptions, and therefore liable to disappoint those who entertain them. But science habitually assumes, at least as a working hypothesis, that general rules which have exceptions can be replaced by general rules which have no exceptions. 'Unsupported bodies in air fall' is a general rule to which balloons and aeroplanes are exceptions. But the laws of motion and the law of gravitation, which account for the fact that most bodies fall, also account for the fact that balloons and aeroplanes can rise; thus the laws of motion and the law of gravitation are not subject to these exceptions.

K

The belief that the sun will rise tomorrow might be falsified if the earth came suddenly into contact with a large body which destroyed its rotation; but the laws of motion and the law of gravitation would not be infringed by such an event.. The business of science is to find uniformities, such as the laws of motion and the law of gravitation, to which, so far as our experience extends, there are no exceptions. In this search science has been remarkably successful, and it may be conceded that such uniformities have held hitherto. This brings us back to the question: have we any reason, assuming that they have always held in the past, to suppose that they will hold in the future?

It has been argued that we have reason to know that the future will resemble the past, because what was the future has constantly become the past, and has always been found to resemble the past, so that we really have experience of the future, namely of times which were formerly future, which we may call past futures. But such an argument really begs the very question at issue. We have experience of past futures, but not of future futures, and the question is: will future futures resemble past futures? This question is not to be answered by an argument which starts from past futures alone. We have therefore still to seek for some principle which shall enable us to know that the future will follow the same laws as the past.

The reference to the future in this question is not essential. The same question arises when we apply the laws that work in our experience to past things of which we have no experience – as, for example, in geology, or in theories as to the origin of the Solar System. The question we really have to ask is: 'When two things have been found to be often associated, and no instance is known of the one occurring without the other, does the occurrence of one of the two, in a fresh instance, give any good ground for expecting the other?' On our answer to this question must depend the validity of the whole of our expectations as to the future, the whole of the results obtained by induction, and in fact practically all the beliefs upon which our daily life is based.

It must be conceded, to begin with, that the fact that two things have been found often together and never apart does not, by itself, suffice to *prove* demonstratively that they will be found together in the next case we examine. The most we can hope is that the oftener things are found together, the more probable it becomes that they will be found together another time, and that, if they have been found together often enough, the probability will amount *almost* to certainty. It can never quite reach certainty, because we know that in spite of frequent repetitions there some-times is a failure at the last, as in the case of the chicken whose neck is wrung. Thus probability is all we ought to seek.

It might be urged, as against the view we are advocating, that we know all natural phenomena to be subject to the reign of law, and that sometimes, on the basis of observation, we can see that only one law can possibly fit the facts of the case. Now to this view there are two answers. The first is that, even if *some* law which has no exceptions applies to our case, we can never, in practice, be sure that we have discovered that law and not one to which there are exceptions. The second is that the reign of law would seem to be itself only probable, and that our belief that it will hold in the future, or in unexamined cases in the past, is itself based upon the very principle we are examining.

The principle we are examining may be called the *principle of induction*, and its two parts may be stated as follows:

(*a*) When a thing of a certain sort A has been found to be associated with a thing of a certain other sort B, and has never been found dissociated from a thing of the sort B, the greater the number of cases in which A and B have been associated, the greater is the probability that they will be associated in a fresh case in which one of them is known to be present.

(*b*) Under the same circumstances, a sufficient number of cases of association will make the probability of a fresh association nearly a certainty, and will make it approach certainty without limit.

As just stated, the principle applies only to the verification of our expectation in a single fresh instance. But we want also to know that there is a probability in favour of the general law that things of the sort A are *always* associated with things of the sort B, provided a sufficient number of cases of association are known, and no cases of failure of association are known. The probability of the general law is obviously less that the probability of the particular case, since if the general law is true, the particular case must also be true, whereas the particular case may be true with-out the general law being true. Nevertheless the probability of the general law is increased by repetitions, just as the probability of the particular case is. We may therefore repeat the two parts of our principle as regards the general law, thus:

(*a*) The greater the number of cases in which a thing of the sort A has been found associated with a thing of the sort B, the more probable it is (if no cases of failure of association are known) that A is always associated with B.

(*b*) Under the same circumstances, a sufficient number of cases of the association of A with B will make it nearly certain that A is always associated with B, and will make this general law approach certainty without limit.

It should be noted that probability is always relative to certain data. In our case, the data are merely the known cases of co-existence of A and B. There may be other data, which *might* be taken into account, which would gravely alter the probability. For example, a man who had seen a great many white swans might argue, by our principle, that on the data it was *probable* that all swans were white, and this might be a perfectly sound argument. The argument is not disproved by the fact that some swans are black, because a thing may very well happen in spite of the fact that some data render it improbable. In the case of the swans, a man might know that colour is a very variable characteristic in many species of animals, and that, therefore, an induction as to colour is peculiarly liable to error. But this knowledge would be a fresh datum, by no means proving that the probability relatively to our previous data had been wrongly estimated. The fact, there-fore, that things often fail to fulfil our expectations is no evidence that our expectations will not *probably* be fulfilled in a given case or a given class of cases. Thus our inductive principle is at any rate not capable of being *disproved* by an appeal to experience.

The inductive principle, however, is equally incapable of being *proved* by an appeal to experience. Experience might conceivably confirm the inductive principle as regards the cases that have been already examined; but as regards unexamined cases, it is the inductive principle alone that can justify any inference from what has been examined to what has not been examined. All arguments which, on the basis of experience, argue as to the future or the unexperienced parts of the past or present, assume the inductive principle; hence we can never use experience to prove the inductive principle without begging the question. Thus we must either accept the inductive principle on the ground of its intrinsic evidence, or forgo all justification of our expectations about the future. If the principle is unsound, we have no reason to expect the sun to rise tomorrow, to expect bread to be more nourishing than a stone, or to expect that if we throw ourselves off the roof we shall fall. When we see what looks like our best friend approaching us, we shall have no reason to suppose that his body is not inhabited by the mind of our worst enemy or of some total stranger. All our conduct is based upon associations which have worked in the past, and which we therefore regard as likely to work in the future; and this likelihood is dependent for its validity upon the inductive principle.

The general principles of science, such as the belief in the reign of law, and the belief that every event must have a cause, are as completely dependent upon the inductive principle as are the beliefs of daily life. All such general principles are believed because mankind have found innumerable instances of their truth and no instances of their falsehood. But this affords no evidence for their truth in the future, unless the inductive principle is assumed.

Thus all knowledge which, on a basis of experience, tells us something about what is not experienced, is based upon a belief which experience can neither confirm nor confute, yet which, at least in its more concrete applications, appears to be as firmly rooted in us as many of the facts of experience. The existence and justification of such beliefs – for the inductive principle, as we shall see, is not the only example – raises some of the most difficult and most debated problems of philosophy.

Further Readings

RUSSELL

'The Relation of Sense-Data to Physics' in *Mysticism and Logic*
Our Knowledge of the External World, especially Lecture 3
Human Knowledge: Its Scope and Limits, especially Part 6
My Philosophical Development, chapters 1, 2, 11, 12, 16

OTHER AUTHORS

Austin, J. L., *Sense and Sensibilia*, chapters 1–5 (Oxford University
    Press 1962)
Ayer, A. J., *The Problem of Knowledge*, chapters 1–3 (Penguin
    1956)
Ayer, A. J., *Russell*, pp. 72–87, 93–102 (Fontana 1972)
Moore, G. E., *Philosophical Papers*, chapters 2, 7, 10 (Allen &
    Unwin 1959)
Salmon, W. C., *The Foundations of Scientific Inference* (University
    of Pittsburgh 1966)
Warnock, G. J., *English Philosophy Since 1900*, chapters 1–6
    Oxford University Press 1958)
Watling, J., *Bertrand Russell*, pp. 76–93 (Oliver & Boyd 1970)
Wittgenstein, L., *On Certainty* (Blackwell 1969)

Bibliography

This bibliography is by no means exhaustive: Russell produced over seventy books and pamphlets during as many years. I have added a list of books about Russell by other writers, and indicated with an asterisk those that should prove most useful for the beginner.

RUSSELL'S SOCIAL AND POLITICAL WORKS
(All books published by Allen & Unwin)

German Social Democracy (1896, 2nd edn 1965)
Principles of Social Reconstruction (1916)
Political Ideals (1917, 2nd edn 1963)
Roads to Freedom (1918)
The Practice and Theory of Bolshevism (1920, 2nd edn 1949)
The Problem of China (1922)
The Prospects of Industrial Civilisation, with Dora Russell (1923)
On Education (1926)
Sceptical Essays (1928, 2nd edn 1935)
Marriage and Morals (1929)
The Conquest of Happiness (1930)
Education and the Social Order (1932, 7th edn 1970)
Freedom and Organisation 1814–1914 (1934)
In Praise of Idleness (1935)
Which Way to Peace? (1936)
Power: A New Social Analysis (1938)
Authority and the Individual (1949)
Unpopular Essays (1950)
New Hopes for a Changing World (1951)
The Impact of Science on Society (1952)
Human Society in Ethics and Politics (1954)
Why I am Not a Christian (1957)
Common Sense and Nuclear Warfare (1959)
Has Man a Future? (1961)
Unarmed Victory (1963)
War Crimes in Vietnam (1967)

RUSSELL'S PHILOSOPHICAL WORKS

A Critical Exposition of the Philosophy of Leibniz (Cambridge University Press 1900, 2nd edn Allen & Unwin 1937)

The Principles of Mathematics (Cambridge University Press 1903, 2nd edn Allen & Unwin 1937)

Principia Mathematica, with A. N. Whitehead (3 vols, Cambridge University Press 1910, 1912, 1913)

Philosophical Essays (Allen & Unwin 1910, revised edn 1966)

The Problems of Philosophy (Oxford University Press 1959)

Our Knowledge of the External World (Allen & Unwin 1914, 3rd edn 1926)

Mysticism and Logic (Allen & Unwin 1917)

Introduction to Mathematical Philosophy (Allen & Unwin 1919)

The Analysis of Mind (Allen & Unwin 1921)

The Analysis of Matter (Kegan Paul 1927, 2nd edn Allen & Unwin 1954)

An Outline of Philosophy (Allen & Unwin 1927)

An Inquiry into Meaning and Truth (Allen & Unwin 1940)

History of Western Philosophy (Allen & Unwin 1946, 2nd edn 1961)

Human Knowledge: Its Scope and Limits (Allen & Unwin 1948)

Logic and Knowledge: Essays 1901–50, edited by R. C. Marsh (Allen & Unwin 1956)

My Philosophical Development (Allen & Unwin 1959)

OTHER WORKS BY RUSSELL

The ABC of Atoms (Kegan Paul 1923)

The ABC of Relativity (Allen & Unwin 1925, 3rd edn 1969)

The Scientific Outlook (Allen & Unwin 1931, 2nd edn 1949)

The Amberley Papers, with Patricia Russell (2 vols, Hogarth Press 1937, 2nd edn Allen & Unwin 1966)

Portraits from Memory (Allen & Unwin 1956)

The Basic Writings of Bertrand Russell, edited by Robert E. Egner and Lester E. Denonn (Allen & Unwin 1961) (a collection of papers and extracts on various subjects)

The Autobiography of Bertrand Russell (3 vols, Allen & Unwin 1967, 1968, 1969)

The Collected Stories of Bertrand Russell, edited by B. Feinberg (Allen & Unwin 1972) (Russell's fictional writings)

BOOKS ABOUT RUSSELL (BIOGRAPHICAL)

Crawshay-Williams, Rupert, *Russell Remembered* (Oxford University Press 1970)

Feinberg, B. and Kasrils, R., *Bertrand Russell's America*, vol I., 1896–1945 (Allen & Unwin 1973)

Hardy, G. H., *Bertrand Russell and Trinity* (Cambridge University Press 1970)

*Wood, Alan, *Bertrand Russell, the Passionate Sceptic* (Allen & Unwin 1957)

BOOKS ABOUT RUSSELL'S PHILOSOPHY

*Ayer, A. J., *Russell* (Fontana 1972); *Russell and Moore: The Analytical Heritage* (Macmillan 1971)

Eames, Elizabeth R., *Bertrand Russell's Theory of Knowledge* (Allen & Unwin 1969)

Jager, R., *The Development of Bertrand Russell's Philosophy* (Allen & Unwin 1972)

Park, J., *Bertrand Russell on Education* (Allen & Unwin 1964)

Pears, D. F., *Bertrand Russell and the British Tradition in Philosophy* (Fontana 1967); (ed.), *Bertrand Russell* (Doubleday 1972); *Russell's Logical Atomism* (Fontana 1972)

Schilpp, P. (ed.), *The Philosophy of Bertrand Russell* (The Library of Living Philosophers, Cambridge University Press 1944)

Schoenman, R. (ed.), *Bertrand Russell, Philosopher of the Century* (Allen & Unwin 1967)

*Watling, John, *Bertrand Russell* (Oliver & Boyd 1970)

Index